First Look Book
2005/2006

Humdrumming
First Look Book
2005/2006

Edited By Guy Adams

Humdrumming Ltd.
75 Withermoor Road
Bournemouth, Dorset
BH9 2QN

This Paperback Edition 2005

First published in Great Britain by Humdrumming 2005

The Opening 'Storm' Text © 2005 by James Christie
The Imagineer Text © 2005 by Gregory Ashe
Earth Text © 2005 by Guy Adams
More Than This Text © 2005 by Guy Adams
The Organization Text © 2005 by Guy Adams
Songs From The Road Text © 2005 by Guy Adams
Going The Other Way From Home Text © 2005 by Steve Newman
Putting on Plays Text © 2005 by Steve Newman
A Christmas Carve Up Text © 2005 by Steve Newman & Laurence Buxton
Cromwell: The Diary of a Play Text © 2005 by Laurence Buxton

Earth and *A Christmas Carve Up* originally featured in the short story anthology 'Upon The Midnight Clear' from KIC edited by Guy Adams

Songs From The Road and *Putting On Plays* were originally written for the online theatre magazine, The Boards - www.theboards.bc.ca

Cover design © 2005 by Lee Thompson

The above writers assert the moral right to be
established as the creators of this work.

All rights reserved. No part of this book may be used or reproduced in any manner whatsoever without written permission from the authors, except in the case of brief quotations embodied in critical articles or reviews.

All characters in this publication are fictitious and any resemblance to any real persons, living or dead, is purely coincidental.

This book is sold subject to the condition that it shall not, by way of trade or otherwise, be lent, re-sold, hired out or otherwise circulated without the publishers prior consent, in any fom of binding or cover other than that in which it is published and without a similar condition including this contition being imposed on the subsequent purchaser.

Published 2005 by Humdrumming
www.humdrumming.co.uk

ISBN 1-905532-04-0
ISBN 978-1-905532-04-9

Printed by Antony Rowe Ltd in the United Kingdom

Contents

Who are we?   7

Fiction
   Earth   11
   More Than This   21
   The Opening   31
   The Imagineer   45
   Swann & Parker: A Christmas Carve-Up   49

Theatre
   Songs From The Road   61
   Cromwell: The Diary of a Play   63
   Putting on Plays   67

Serials
   Ernest Hemingway: Going The Other Way From Home   81
   The Organization   85

Meet The Humdrumming Crew   89

Editor's Note

As will become clear over the next eighty pages this is an overview of Humdrumming's output for the next six months or so: basically, books that have been commissioned and/or published *now*. It is, by no means, a definitive shape for the future. Currently our output is split very distinctly into fiction (much of which has a fantasy edge) and theatre. In the pipeline, however, are projects as diverse as 'Blackjack' a pulp crime magazine, photographic books, horror westerns and even, dare I say, erotica.

Humdrumming has no limits, we have no single hook we wish to hang our publishing hat on. What we are is a place for diverse writers and artists to create exciting personal projects and produce work that will be as dear to them as it hopefully will be with their readers.

It just so happens that your establishing body of authors rather *like* fantasy and may have a theatrical background.

Okay?

Okay.

'We will not be pushed, stamped, filed, indexed, briefed, debriefed or numbered. Our life is our own.'

Sorry.

Guy Adams.

WHO ARE WE?

To put it ostentatiously: A new world of publishing.

To put it simply: A small publishing company set up by professional writers and designers to provide a valid and exciting shop front for their abilities.

In today's publishing industry it can be difficult to find a market for new work. There's a tendency to play safe, to mine proven talent or encourage new talent to emulate the styles and subjects that companies – and, to a degree, bookstores – know are effortlessly commercial.

We're generalising of course, but you get our drift.

It is in this environment that Humdrumming was developed. All of us here have, to varying levels, worked as freelancers in the mainstream publishing industry. One night (and let's be honest it involved wine, these things always do) we got to wondering whether it would be viable to create a small scale publishing house that would specialise in interesting creator-owned projects. Books we'd always wanted to write but couldn't find a mainstream market for, books that were personal and that we wanted to craft in our own way, books that we wanted to do for *fun*.

It would have to be extremely professional; this was, after all, our heart and soul we were pushing out into the market place. Everything would have to be our best possible work, presented in the best possible way. But it would be *ours*. To do with as we wished. Think of it as an independent music label but for books if you like. A place where we could experiment, where we could run with our ideas and not have to limit ourselves with thoughts of contracts and markets. Ultimately, you see, it seemed to us that if we wanted to create something then there would automatically be a market for it – if an idea fascinated us then, by the nature of odds, there would be a reader somewhere.

It could even be you.

It would be risky of course: we would be biting off a considerable amount of work and the need to constantly swap hats with one another, writer, editor, designer… It could be financially terrifying too, but these days there are viable quality printing methods that can help ease that burden. Nothing would leave our hands that was anything less than the highest possible standard, of that we were determined. But, could we maintain quality and artistic intent without sending ourselves bankrupt and/or insane?

Well, you already know the answer to that don't you?

Because you're looking at it.

Welcome aboard.

FICTION

Earth
Guy Adams

I woke up this morning to find a woman in my bed and I still don't know what to do about it. At the time I slipped from under my side of the duvet and crept out of the room, not willing to make any decisions just yet. Besides, I had work to do - make a few calls, y'know, the usual.

I was on the street by ten, cold air and crowded pavements. Everywhere you went the lampposts and shop fronts were draped with lights and tinsel. Each store you went into was playing the same CD - Roy Wood was wishing it could be Christmas everyday over and over again. People fought, laughed, cried. Children yelled. Car horns barked. Come eleven I was hiding out in a coffee shop wishing the World would have the decency to shut its damned mouth for a second. Just enough to give me room to breathe.

And all the while, thinking about that woman lying in my bed.

Christmas is a crazy time for me; business gets kind of weird. A lot of my regulars drop off the radar for a while, bitten by the Jesus bug. Guilt and a newfound sense of religious propriety make them lie low. They'd be back of course, nobody dropped out forever, just wait until January had crushed all the soul out of them; the phone would ring soon enough.

Christmas also brought me new faces, those that would never normally score. This time of the year just gets to some people, people sick of all that good living family bullshit being rammed down their throats at every possible opportunity. You can only take so much perfection being thrown at you; after a bit it begins to feel like someone's laughing at you. That's when they come to me.

I can give them something to make them better, to fill a hole in themselves or put one in someone else. That's what I do.

I deal in magick.

Nothing major as a rule - though I've dabbled in some heavy stuff from time to time - just the usual boring clichés. Love spells, curses, uppers and downers. Your basic Urban Voudoun. Incantation stuff.

I also sell a few charms, texts, objects of 'power', all that hokey rigmarole.

What can I say? It keeps the roof over my head.

I finished my coffee and headed up west where I was due to meet a client at half eleven. His name's Jeff (I don't swap surnames, most of my clients like to feel there's a bit of anonymity), works in advertising or some other soul-sapping crap. Decent guy, for an office monkey anyway. He doesn't play with the big stuff, always pays cash - bread and butter in other words.

I met him at a little Sushi place across the road from his office. One of those chrome and plastic seat affairs, low comfort - high price.

"Hi Danny," he said, strolling through the door with some other guy I've never met. If anyone else had tried this with me they'd have been handed their brain on one of the little sushi plates that revolve around the counter. You had to be careful in my line of business. Still Jeff was no idiot, if he thought the guy was safe then he probably was.

"Jeff. Who's your friend?"

"This is Tommy, works across the way from me. Thought you might be able to fix him up with some stuff."

"Yeah?" I shuffled in my seat a little, trust or no trust this wasn't how I liked to do business. I pointed at the couple of seats facing mine. "Well then keep your voice down and park yourselves. What sort of stuff are we talking about here?"

Tommy was middle aged, his gut pressing at his shirt buttons from the inside. Hair was thinning, forehead shiny. He kept rubbing his hands together though through nervousness or excitement I couldn't really tell. Both probably.

"He's got a thing about one of the girls in accounts..." Jeff said, chuckling like a schoolboy.

"He can tell me himself, can't you Tommy?" I went to light a cigarette then remembered the place was non-smoking so I just fidgeted with the pack.

Tommy sighed and looked around to see if anyone was watching us. They weren't, for all my moaning about Jeff mouthing off I'm not stupid, I'd placed a discretion charm around the table before they even came in. Anyone listening wouldn't pick up a word.

"It's like Jeff says, Tina's her name."

"Okay. What exactly is it you want from me?"

"I just want something to make her like me."

I sighed, one day somebody would sing a different song.

"I can't make her *like* you Tommy, not really. I can make her *think* she likes you but that really isn't the same thing is it? You sure you know what you're doing with this?"

He looked at me then and I could see in his vacant little pig eyes that he knew damn well what he wanted. Christ, for all their talk of 'love' or 'like' it always boils down to the same thing. They just want to get their end away without recrimination, the magickal form of Rohypnol.

Which made me think of the woman in my bed; which, in turn, took all the fight out of me. Hell, let 'em do what they want.

"Yeah, I can fix you up. It won't be cheap but it'll get you what you want. I'm going to need some stuff from you though; I'll do you a list."

I scribbled in the little notebook I always carried, all the usual mythic crap, lock of hair, recent photo, you know the sort of thing.

"What about you Jeff? The usual is it?"

Jeff was your esteem junkie, the other best seller in my stock. I sold him a small charm that he wears around his neck, it doesn't make people like him but it sure as hell makes him like himself - which tends to lead to the same thing in the end doesn't it? In all fairness I was running a bit of a con on Jeff, the charm worked, that was fine but I had him under the impression that it needed replacing every couple of months - just to keep the sales up y'know? Kind of dirty I'll admit but he can afford it. Besides, it makes the thing seem more potent somehow, as if it's kicking out a lot of juice.

"Yeah, thanks pal." He winked and passed me a thick envelope, which I swapped for one from my own pocket.

Nice and smooth. I turned to Tommy.

"Once you get everything on my shopping list you give me a call and I'll see what I can sort out."

"Okay, thanks"

"Don't thank me until I've done something to earn it."

I got to my feet.

"Wait a minute," Jeff said, pulling another envelope from his pocket. "This is for you."

I took it and tore it open. Inside there was a Christmas card. One of those arty minimalist affairs, black and white close up of a holly leaf or some shit. I threw it on the table.

"I'm not your friend Jeff. Save it for someone who is."

The poor bastard was stunned, and I felt a pang of guilt as I walked out. Truth is he'd caught me on a tender subject. I don't do Christmas. Hate it. I'm one of those bitter people I mentioned earlier. Not that he could have known that.

I nearly walked back in to apologise but I was still feeling angry and decided I'd only screw it up. Hell with it, I'd call him later.

I walked around the block a couple of times, just to calm down and then rang my next client. Joe the Taxi he calls himself. Guess he must have liked the song. He really is a cab driver, which is pretty damned useful at times. He gives me a lift to where I need to be and we conduct our business at the same time.

It took him about ten minutes to get over to me, during which I smoked a cigarette and tried to decide what to do about the woman in my flat. I was still none the wiser as I climbed into the back of his cab and gave him the directions.

"How's it going Danny?" He asked as we made our way along all the little side streets and back alleys that you only ever see from the back of a cab. God help you if you ever try to find them on your own, you'll be lost within seconds. This is Cabbie Magic

"Yeah... bad time of year Joe. You know how it is."

"Caroline yeah?"

"Yeah."

Joe knew all about Caroline. When I'd got the call he was the one that ran me to the hospital. Double quick time too I have to say, not that it did any good. She was dead on arrival. Not many people walk away from the wrong end of a drunk in a Mercedes and Caroline was no exception. That had been two Christmases ago, which would be why I lacked a certain seasonal spirit.

"It's tough Danny, I know."

He did too, though his wife was still alive - just living in Birmingham with an Optician and their two kids. I thought about telling him what had happened that morning (he was as close as I got to a friend these days). I decided not to, at least not until I knew what I was going to do about it.

"How about you Joe? What can I do you for?"

"Ah... just a bit more Karkash Root, my supplies getting kind of low."

"No problem," I'd guessed as much and had brought a half-pound with me on the off chance.

Joe's got any interesting solution to the loneliness thing you see, he builds homunculi. They look like women, move like women, feel like women. Difference is: they're not real; just dummies - dolls. The Karkash Root comes in from West Africa; it's the base ingredient in giving the things an appearance of life.

I'll be honest, I've tried it, but it really didn't work out, they have a lifeless look in their eyes that freaks me out, that and the idea of them just falling apart after a few weeks. It's good for Joe though, he can't bear the idea of starting again, hasn't the confidence, at least this way he can feel like there's somebody around, someone to care for him.

I dumped the package on his passenger seat as we pulled up.

"Call it a present." I said.

"Hey, are you sure?"

"Yeah, don't worry about it."

"Thanks, look after yourself okay?"

I smiled, though I'll admit it was forced, and waved him off.

I strolled down the street a little way, grabbing another smoke. I was going to make Billy the last call of the day - I really did have to sort the situation out back home - but I always made sure I arrived a little late. It didn't pay to have him think I needed him too much. You see, Billy was my supplier - one of them anyway. I know some stuff, I'm a fair Magus on an everyday level, but when it comes to more specialist requirements I give Billy a call. He's a bit of a theatrical prick - swans about the place in a caftan reeking of incense - and he will try and convince you he's part of a long Houngan line from Haiti, whereas I have it on good authority he's a Brixton boy through and through. There's no denying he knows his subject though and for the stuff I don't want to get too involved in he's my best contact.

I paused outside a flower shop while I finished my cigarette. There was a large bunch of white lilies in the window. Caroline had always loved lilies. I used to buy her a bunch every now and then, not as often as I should I'm sure, but y'know - *regularly*.

The last time I'd bought some for her was when they put her in the ground.

I dropped my cigarette and trod on it before walking past a few more houses and up to Billy's front door.

I rang the bell and pulled at my coat, Christ but it was getting cold out here.

Billy opened the door and the wave of Patchouli that hit me in the face nearly had me throwing up on his front step.

"Ah…" his voice rumbled, "Danny my son, it is good to see you."

"Yeah, you too Billy, let me in would you I'm freezing out here."

He stepped out of the way so that I could get inside. It was still something of a struggle; Billy's a big man. Likes his cakes.

I shuffled through to his front room and took a seat on his sofa.

"Get you a drink Danny?"

"Yeah, whatever's going."

I started to warm up, he had the gas fire up on full and, despite the skulls and horns he had hanging everywhere, I was getting quite comfy as he passed me a beer.

"So," he said, dropping into a reclining armchair with a crash, "how did it go?"

"What?" I asked.

"The thing, last week, the incantation."

"Oh come on," I said sipping at my beer, "You know I'm not a user, I passed that on and I've had no complaints."

He looked at me for a few moments.

"Not a user huh?"

"Damn right, I strictly deal - you know that."

He took a drink of his beer and nodded.

"Whatever you say Danny, whatever you say."

I was tensing up, hadn't been expecting this. I'd just wanted to place a couple of big orders and then get home. I needed to get home…

(Because there was a woman in my bed and I didn't know what to do about it)

…and keep my head down until the World got over this stupid Christmas thing and we could all get on with business as normal.

He looked at me again and I could tell he was weighing up whether to push the subject. Eventually he just nodded again and took another mouthful of beer.

"So what can I get for you?"

I took out my notepad and reeled off a few orders I'd taken over the last couple of days, glad to just get the business over and done with. He made a few notes of his own and finished his beer.

"You want another one?" he asked.

I did, but not here.

"I'm fine, I've got to be getting on - few more things to do before everybody vanishes for a couple of days."

"Yeah, know what you mean. Okay, I'll give you a call when I can fix you up."

"Great," I got to my feet and he led me back to the front door.

"Danny?" he said as I was walking down his path, shivering against the sudden drop in temperature.

"Yeah?" I turned to look at him, hands in my coat pockets, shoulders hunched.

"Make sure you know what you're doing."

I was going to question him, demand to know what he meant - I hate all that enigmatic crap he throws about, that sort of thing's for the punters not me - but he closed the door before I had chance. I stayed there for a moment, just stood on his path, then swore under my breath and headed back along the street.

The shop windows were trying to convince me it was a good time of the year: posters for greetings cards, twinkling fairy lights, great tubs of wrapping paper and spinning baubles. I didn't believe them.

I was about to call a cab when I saw the neon of a small bar. A quick drink would do me good I felt. Just a little more breathing space before I had to go home.

It turned out to be several and the sky was beginning to get dark by the time I stumbled out.

I called my cab and strolled up and down the street while I waited, trying to decide what to do.

When the car came I was feeling a lot better, more resolved. It was understandable that I'd been nervous; it'd been two years for god's sake. Still, sometimes you've just got to do it haven't you?

By the time I stepped in through my flat door it was dark, the flashing Christmas lights from the street outside pulsing through my windows and throwing their red, orange and green across my walls.

There's a woman in my bed.

I went to flick on the hall light then drew short. It was so quiet, had she gone? Left me? Had I offended her by dashing out this morning?

I walked through to the bedroom and paused in the doorway as the second hand lights from outside lit up the shape in bed. She was still here. Still in my bed.

I walked slowly towards her holding out the Lilies I'd dashed back to the shop for while waiting for my taxi.

"Merry Christmas love." I said, surprised at how natural the words sounded.

The shape moved and sat up in bed, a pulse of red catching the side of her face. She was a bit of a mess, he hair splayed about. Still, I'd expected that, Billy had warned me about that.

I sat on the bed and held the flowers out to her. When she didn't take them I just laid them her lap.

"Lilies love, your favourite."

She didn't say anything, did she even remember?

"Caroline love, remember? Lilies?"
"Lilies?" She whispered, her voice rough and dry.
"That's right!"

And I took her in my arms and kissed her, inhaling deep the musty smell of earth.

Danny Fix appears in the deadbeat series of adventures.

Deadbeat
By Guy Adams
ISBN 1-905532-02-4 - Available Now

"I think you're missing something, what did you notice about the woman in the coffin? ...She was breathing. Not a common habit amongst the dead."

It's the middle of the night and, in a dark suburban churchyard, a group of men are loading a coffin into the back of a transit van.

But why would you be taking a full coffin away from a graveyard and, more importantly, why is the occupant still breathing?

The matter obviously needs thorough investigation by the best, most capable authorities.

Which is a pity as the only two witnesses are a pair of drunken ex-theatricals with reasons of their own to avoid the police.

Tom Harris (nightclub owner) and Max Jackson (habitual barfly) are on the case.

God help us...

Deadbeat *is the first in a series of adventures set the secret underbelly of contemporary London, a place where the dead walk, magic can be bought on street corners and anything is possible.*

Frankly, it's just like every other Pulp Crime/Horror/Zombie/Comedy/Thriller you've ever read.

Deadbeat : The Dogs of Waugh
By Guy Adams
ISBN 1-905532-14-8 - Coming Soon

"High on life..."

There's a new drug running rife amongst the Undead community. Once ingested it simulates all of the symptoms of the living, faster pulse, perspiration, the intoxicating rush of blood through your veins...

Not that Max or Tom would be stupid enough to try it of course, they're far to busy smashing their senses to a pulp working their way though Deadbeat's new cocktail menu.

But when people start vanishing from the Soho streets and some of their customers disrupt big band nights by keeling over dead for the second time they decide it might be worth looking into, if only to stop profits dropping too far.

Which, in a lifetime of bad decisions, may rank as their worst yet.

MORE THAN THIS

GUY ADAMS

An excerpt from...

MORE THAN THIS
BY GUY ADAMS - ISBN 1-905532-05-9

"There was something in the water"

Kiss me quick and squeeze me slow, there's something amiss in the crumbling seaside resort of Gravestown: Children are vanishing and nobody can understand how.

Gregory Ashe watches them go, sees them hanging from their tatty 'wanted' pictures and the wilting bouquets of flowers left by well wishers. Like most thirteen year olds he feels it's nothing to do with him, he's far too busy with his face in a book and a head full of dreams.

Then, amongst the seaweed and shingle, a solitary foot is washed up and the violence begins.

Gravestown is infected. People are beginning to lose their minds, changing, becoming other. Blood is spilt, over and over and over...

Through it all the waves roll and, in the dark building on the cliff tops, the lunatics howl by the light of their moon.

Slowly the safe walls of reality are crumbling and it seems nobody can stop it.

Nobody that is except The Magician, a man who takes young Gregory under his wing and shows him how hollow those dreams of his really are, a man with more than just spare decks of cards hidden up his sleeve.

Gregory's never been in so much danger...

A dark fantasy laced with humour and terror. More Than This is a fast paced journey from innocence to maturity, fear to hope, heaven to hell. Exciting, horrifying and filled with the sort of imagination, escapism and, above all, magic you remember from books you read as a child - magic you thought lost.

Like many bastards Gravestown was born while the father was elsewhere.

Scrabbling into life on its own insignificant wedge of dreary coastline with as much real hope of a bright future as a retarded orphan. The odds were against it before the first echoes of birth trauma had faded.

Hopes had been high; it was to be a place of commerce and affluence, a place of quiet reflection, beauty and tranquillity; a place where all who visited would dream of being able to remain there in perpetuity.

Within half a century it was banging out its 'beauty' with all the pride and respect of a cheap whore on a back street trying to make that month's rent.

The plans were traditional enough, pier and promenade leading back to a small grid of streets lined with shops and hostelries to cater to the illustrious visitors it had hoped to attract. A sizeable park and rose garden was plotted for one end of the promenade while a bandstand and solarium would stand proud at the other. When the money dried up and the attention waned the park remained plain and the bandstand jerry rigged. No one cared anymore; the town was beginning to live up to its name. The original, rather egocentric nomenclature of Walgravestown became Gravestown through repetition and carelessness; give it another few decades of consonantal shift and Gravestone will be the name on all the signs (although the wit of many a spray painting youth will beat it by a good few years).

All of which is not to say that the town was a complete failure, just that the benchmark had to be shifted a little; a microwave meal may not bear scrutiny next to a cordon bleu plate but it'll still fill your gut. Money changed hands, good times were had and many people filled the houses that fell back from the centre wave after wave.

For a while at least…

- 2 -

It was the sound that distracted Karen from washing her hands.

High and insistent, like the squeal of a rodent. It took her some time to locate it as the spinning wheel of the air vent in her kitchen window, whipped into a frenzy by the building storm outside. Round and round it went, frantic, urgent, incessant. She watched it for a while before a growing thirst drew her to the kettle and kitchen tap.

She stabbed at the kettle with the carving knife she hadn't been aware of carrying, paused for a moment, confused, then put the knife down and picked the kettle up safely to fill it with water. It nearly slipped in her grip; so slick were her palms with blood. She gripped the handle tighter, filled it from the running tap and then placed the kettle on the stove.

Curious, she thought, as she glanced at her hands.
Now where did all that come from?

It slipped her mind for a moment as she lit the gas and listened to the reassuring rush of the blue flame. Then she noticed the continuing flow of water from the tap and turned to shut it off, balking for a moment at the red smears all over the handle. *What a mess.* She picked up a cloth to wipe it away, pausing as she saw the blood all over her hands again. Tutting to herself she rubbed her hands under the cold water, watching the congealing liquid drip and dilute as it flowed down the plughole. That too was distracting for a few minutes, watching the water become clearer and clearer as the blood washed away. Hadn't she heard that water flowed in the opposite direction in Australia? Anti-clockwise. What would they think of next?

The kettle was beginning to whistle so she turned off the tap, wiping it carefully with the cloth, and returned to making a drink.

She turned off the gas, reached for a tea bag and cup, noticed the bloodstained knife on the worktop and flinched away. What was that doing there? Its blade was large and very sharp, ideal for a Sunday Roast, but you did have to be careful; she had nicked herself a couple of times on it over the years, usually when she had been rushing to get dinner ready for Jimmy on his return from the pub. Blood had been drawn certainly but never in those quantities. She checked her hands for cuts but found none.

Curious, she thought, as she stared at the blood on the blade.
Now where did all that come from?

It couldn't stay there, what if one of the kids found it?
They could hurt themselves.

The kids.

Panicking, she picked up the knife, ran out into the hall and up the stairs to the nursery. Well, they called it a nursery but there were few toys, just a pair of cots, hand me downs and the sort of cheap stuffed nonsenses that she could afford with the change Jimmy gave her from his beer money. They always said that they would make it nicer one day. Decorate it a little, maybe even a mobile to hang over the cots, she'd seen a lovely one, a moon and stars. She was sure they would like it. Little David was always so curious, reaching for everything he didn't understand, and Susan liked bright things. Shiny, sparkly things, always cooing and chuckling at the necklace Karen wore, as it swung to and fro from her neck; at the bunch of keys she dangled over the cot sometimes; at the spangle sharp blade of the carving knife she always used for the Sunday Roast. Giggling and burbling, reaching for it with her soft stubbly little fingers.

Curious, she thought, as her eyes followed the arc sprays of blood that spattered the walls of the nursery. *Now where did all that come from?*

My goodness but she was thirsty, she'd kill for a cup of tea. As she turned to leave she caught her reflection in the mirror hung on the facing wall. Her dress was ruined. Blood on her chest, blood on her face, blood in her hair. She brushed a stray length away from her face. Jimmy wouldn't be too happy to catch her looking like that; Jimmy liked things just so.

There was a rattle from the front door. Dear lord, here he was, home already. He'd want a supper, what had she been thinking dawdling like this? She had nothing prepared.

She ran out of the nursery, steadying herself on the doorframe as her heel slipped slightly in a wet patch on the carpet, and ran downstairs. She reached the foot of the stairs as the door opened and Jimmy stumbled in, yanking awkwardly at his keys to rescue them from the lock. He looked up and dropped his jaw in shock at the sight of the crazed woman running toward him. Karen laughed pleasantly and shoved the carving knife she was still holding straight into his open mouth where it tore his tongue in two before puncturing the top of his windpipe and scraping to a halt across the bone in his neck. He fell back, knocking the door closed with the weight of his body. Pushing himself upright, he spiralled around, a loud wet click coming from his mouth as he involuntarily tried to swallow.

Karen skipped into the kitchen, glad that Jimmy didn't seem to be angry with her for not having food ready. Behind her she could hear the high-pitched whistling noises as he struggled to breathe, it confused her for a moment before she glanced at the spinning plastic air vent in the window and remembered. Noticing the kettle on the stove she wondered if he might want a cup of tea with his supper. She picked it up and took it to him in the hall.

She hit him first to the side of the head, splashing boiling water across the flock paper behind him, then once to stomach and finally square into his face where it hammered the knife deeper. He grunted, coughed a spray of blood into her face and slowly dropped to his knees. Finally, he toppled forward and, as his face hit the carpet, there was another gentle crunch as the knife slid further still, the point erupting from the nape of his neck.

She wiped at her face with her hands, trying to clear the blood from her eyes. She was covered; she really should try and clean herself up. Jimmy wouldn't be too happy to catch her looking like this; Jimmy liked things just so.

It was the sound that distracted Karen from washing her hands. High and insistent, like the squeal of a rodent. It took her some time to locate it as the spinning wheel of the air vent in her kitchen window, whipped into frenzy by the building storm outside. Round and round it went, frantic, urgent, incessant. She caught sight of her reflection in the window. Dishevelled and covered in the blood of her family.

Curious, she thought, as she began to cry. *Now where did all that come from?*

-3-

The inherent problem with having a 'kiss me quick' attitude, of course, is that people tend to label you something of a tart.

And, as a knee-jerk response, you can't really blame them. Gravestown set great store in its bright and breezy attitude, in its gaudy spectacle and cheap ale. Arnold Newman, still in firm possession of his chain of Mayoral office and many years from stumbling over a child's severed foot on the beach, once had the bravado to go on record as saying "There are more thrills in Gravestown than there are fleas on a Tinker's trousers". It was an unfortunate comment and one he would take a while to live down, however many times he insisted that it was taken out of context (a shallow defence, even if one assumes there could *be* a context in which Tinker's trousers would sound apposite). It was also something of a lie, or, in the spirit of fairness, exaggeration. True it would depend on your definition of thrill, but there was little in Gravestown to which the word could universally be applied. Yes, there was a funfair during the summer months, a temporary pitch arranged around the bandstand that was filled by the *Bertucci Travelling Carnival!* (The rather excitable brainchild of two Glaswegian brothers whose only link to Italy was that their father had shot some of its residents during the war), but even then the rides were, for the most part, sedate affairs. Little more than a selection of child friendly 'turns' as mutually agreed by the town council and the Brothers Bertucci (neé MacGregor) after a group of Holidaymakers from Wolverhampton had lost a collective eight front teeth during a moment of abandon concerning a speed control on the part of the Waltzers operator. The ultimate upshot of this being the realisation that: there are only so many times an adult can be ferried around a circular track in a fibre glass mock up of a racing car before the Tinker's trousers sound more fun.

Four Penny Arcades were dotted along the front, but again, throwing good money after bad in a desperate attempt to win a stuffed toy elephant has a time limit as far as entertainment goes. Nor did it take even the most novice of gamblers long to realise that all of the fruit machines had been cannily adjusted to the 'rape the customer blind' setting as the amount of times they paid out could be seen as proportionate to the amount of Tuesdays in any given week.

There was the pier of course, but beyond the ranks of shuffling perverts pumping the small fixed telescopes with pennies on the hunt for magnified cleavage and a selection of display boards giving the (selective) history of the town there was little else to occupy you.

Once these opportunities for a wild time were sampled there was little to do except rot your guts with ice cream and candyfloss and stand behind the chipped wooden cut-out on the pier to have your photo taken looking like a fat bastard in an Edwardian bathing suit.

All of which had its devotees of course, these were simpler times and the populace was used to 'making do'. Yet, while other Seaside towns expanded over the years, stealing bright shiny ideas from America and boosting their market, Gravestown stayed pretty much as it was. It made money, but not much. Achieving that desperate air of a terminal patient maintaining a holding pattern, their past faculties becoming ever more diluted, slowly but surely waiting for death.

-4-

If the windows are truly the 'eyes' of a building, then the *Bargainrite Bonanza* didn't see the Molotov cocktail coming as it already been blinded by a well aimed hail of bricks.

The fire lashed across aisles four and five (home ware and cleaning products) and sent a tongue whipping against the back wall where it took hold of a poster advertising two for one on Daz washing powder.

The boys took their seats on the bonnets of the cars parked outside and settled back with a packet of stolen cigarettes.

There were five of them in total: Derren Bright, Luke Handsworthy, Peter Morris (although his friends called him 'Tonto' due to his prodigious buck teeth), Mike Fowler and Colin Reilly (son of Tony Reilly, the pier's medical officer and brief media darling after he'd been the one to bundle the foot up and out of harm's way a few weeks back). It was Derren's birthday, which placed him a clear four months older than the rest.

He was thirteen.

They were waiting by the burning shop for a reason; not only did they want to watch their handiwork grow, they wanted to see what would happen when the fire reached the owner's flat. They were pretty sure that the only way out was via the passage and stairs behind the shop counter, had seen old Brian Greene come and go that way frequently when they had cued to buy sweets from his wife, Eileen, who was commonly behind the till.

He was a little unsteady on his legs these days, the stick he'd reserved for when the weather was damp or there was ice on the paths had been a permanent fixture over the last couple of months. They hadn't expected him to come running at the sound of breaking glass therefore, and there was no way Eileen would be the first face at the strip curtain that led out back, there were mice with braver temperaments. Taking all of this into consideration they had estimated a response time of nearly two minutes, thirty seconds for the shock, another forty or so for the pulling on of a dressing gown and retrieval of his stick, same again for the cautious negotiation of the stairs. It might be even more if he paused to call the police rather than order his wife to do it. Not that it would achieve anything, they'd cut the phone cables along the street before they'd raised their first stone, something Mike had suggested after remembering an episode of Dragnet from a few weeks before.

The flames were getting thoroughly entrenched on the opposite side of the shop to the exit. They hoped the fire wasn't going to get too advanced before Brian made an appearance, that would take all of the fun out of it, there was still a sizeable pile of broken bricks on the pavement in front of them and they were there to be used.

Luke checked his watch; the old man had had his two minutes. As one they shuffled off the bonnets and began to select their favourite weapons. Colin selected according to size, for Peter sharpness was the key.

The strip curtain parted briefly, they heard the old man shout to his wife and, after another few seconds they both made their way onto the shop floor. Bonus. The boys allowed them to clear the passage by a few feet, moving quickly but cautiously towards the front door and broken windows, it would be a tactical error on their part if the couple had darted back out of sight as soon as they realised the boys were still there.

Derren (who had selected a mid-sized brick fragment, shaped bizarrely, he thought, like a poodle's head) went first.

It *was* his birthday after all…

However proficient they were with Balloon Animals, you wouldn't ask a Clown to fit your bathroom.

And therein lay Gravestown's problem: It did what it did but no more. There was no great business, no industry, nothing to fall back on. It was inevitable therefore that should the bottom fall out of its tourist market there would be no keeping the town afloat. There were those that commuted elsewhere for their employment of course, and as long as there were a few of them then someone else would be able to make money by keeping them fed and watered. That covered the backs of the shop owners whose trades were aimed as much at the locals as the tourists. Didn't help you much if you made your crust from hard rock sweets fashioned into amusing shapes though; there are only so many boiled egg or breast shaped fancies a household can legitimately own, even assuming they take the plunge and wipe out their supply by eating them.

New residents of the town looked elsewhere for their income, the dynamics began to shift, Gravestown became less a place you went to, more a place you started *from*. The bus and train service told the story best, all seats full on the way out, empty on the way in.

Which means, whichever way you cut it, it was going to end in tears one way or another.

Jeremy Ashe had had sex twice since the action on the Pier and he was coming to the rather unpleasant conclusion that he wasn't very good at it.

The realisation made him give a dismissive grunt towards the rather sleepy looking Joan and take a stroll along the beach.
After they had given the freak a damn good kicking they had picked up the girls and gone out to walk the streets for a while; hunting for the next thrill, settling for sitting around on the sand when they hadn't found one. Jeremy felt drunk, probably was drunk a little, the Gin in his system had vanished after the pier, adrenaline burning it off very quickly, but he'd had a few sips since. Not many mind, because, truth be told, he felt a little sick. Sick and confused. There were three distinct emotions rolling around his hormone-addled brain; fear, guilt and lastly, god help him, *pride*. It was one thing to know that you'd done something wrong, to be aware deep within your gut that you'd crossed a moral line that just shouldn't be crossed.

It was something else again to realise you'd *liked* it.

There had been a great sense of power, still was, he'd listened to the voice in his head, acted on it, and now the world was a different place because of him. For better or worse was almost immaterial.

He knew it was wrong (*Jesus, so wrong*), but he had to make a choice: to step back from it, to admit his culpability and take the consequences, or to keep going. He knew what he *should* do…

But the voice in his head was still talking and it was getting so hard to think…

Glancing up at the streetlights and the road he saw something coming towards them and all rational thought vanished; vanished to be replaced with something altogether worse: an *idea*.

He ran towards the road, shouting over his shoulder to the gang behind him, still lolling about on the sand, directionless and functionless without him and the voice inside him to light a fire beneath them.

He didn't check to see if they were following, just jumped up on the sea wall and climbed over onto the pavement on the other side. Not even looking to see if there was any traffic, he sprinted across and along to the bus stop where the Number 12 was letting out it's last customer of the night.

He jumped through the closing door and, even while the driver was trying to say that his route was done, just the short hop to the depot and home to bed, he punched him full in the face. Then again, and again, before the man even had time to react. The fourth was the charm, the driver was old and overweight, trapped in his seat, Jeremy however was young and able to put the full weight of his body behind the blows. There was a crack as his knuckles connected with the bridge of the man's nose, sending shards of bone swimming back into grey matter, a spurt of blood from his nostrils and then he slumped back against the driver's side window.

The pain was beginning to grow in Jeremy's hand, but for now, the adrenaline and the excited screaming in his head held it back. He reached for the catch that would release the barrier between them, flipped it open and pulled the driver from his seat, letting his own dead weight send him toppling to the floor of the bus. He then rolled him with his feet, pushing him out of the door and onto the pavement outside where he landed with a puff of air at the feet of Keith and Dave who had caught up with him by now. Looking out of the front windscreen he could see Ann and Joan on the other side of the road, gazing over in sleepy confusion.

"What are you waiting for?" He shouted, "Hop on board."

He clambered into the driver's seat and hunted for the ignition, pulling the barrier closed behind him.

Keith and Dave shared a look, laughed and then cheered as the bus engine roared into life. They waved the girls over and they all clambered on board as Jeremy tried to get a feel for the pedals. Suddenly he paused, aware again of the voice in his head, whispering instructions. God bless the King of Mods, he thought, where would I be without him?

"Where are we going?" Asked Joan as she fell into one of the seats. Jeremy chuckled, pulled out onto the road and slammed down the accelerator.

"Wherever the fuck we want darling, this is the Magic Bus, last stop: Cliff Richard's front lawn."

-7-

All of which begs the question: at what point would it be acceptable to commit euthanasia on a town?

Even acknowledging the inherent difficulty in carrying out the mercy killing we would have to say the patient was really starting to beg for it. There was little hope for long-term survival and little genuine pleasure of life left in its streets. Wouldn't it be the kindest thing in the long run?

Sadly it's not our choice to make, besides if we were to extend the analogy; continue in our anthropomorphosis of town to living being, it seemed to be doing a rather good job of it itself. Much more of this sort of behaviour and it would certainly burn up in an act of self-destruction in very little time at all. Or perhaps it would survive only to be pulled up in front of the courts, maybe even plead diminished responsibility? For there can be little question as the night unfolded, as its streets and houses erupted in violence and chaos, as its populace looked up at the moon outside its window and began to feel an itch deep inside.

Gravestown had become well and truly insane.

The adventure continues in 'More Than This' available from Humdrumming in November 2006.

THE OPENING

JAMES CHRISTIE

An excerpt from...

THE OPENING
BY JAMES CHRISTIE - ISBN 1-905532-03-2

The world spins, mankind goes about its business sure and certain that all is well.

Nothing ever changes, day follows day follows day.

Mankind is so very wrong...

Moving from the mountains of Andalucia to the black ghettos of the Mississippi Delta, from a mysterious encampment in the Negev Desert to the Oaken Groves of Britain's High Druids, Colin Mage, modern day magician, races against time to prevent The Opening... A magical ritual that opens the gates to Hell on Earth.

Even with the Help of people like Michael Fry, The Merlin of Britain, Helen Ross, the Wiccan Priestess from the Scottish glens, Herschall the Jewish shaman with powerful political allies, John Light, one time Satanist turned evangelical Christian and Leon Shapiro, the Mossad agent who has more faith in guns and computers than in mystical beliefs, the odds appear insurmountable.

It is Castillo, an isolated village in Southern Spain, that becomes the battleground for the final conflict between Man and his greatest adversary, and it is only in Castillo that Mage discovers who his true friends are and the appalling extent of his enemy's capacity for pure evil.

Storm

Mage toed and heeled the pedals of the Land Rover and hurled the heavy machine around the impossibly tight corners of Castillo's forbidding one way system. When he intersected with the main street he put his foot down and accelerated up the steep hill towards the town hall and the police station. The rain hammered in a cacophonic din against the roof and the single speed wipers were hard pressed to cope with the deluge of water that exploded against the glass panes of the split windscreen. The Land Rover was in excellent condition for its age, but it was old and lacked the sophistication of later models. The de-mister hissed pathetically and drops of water leaked in from a variety of places – a window panel here, a strained rivet there...

And yet Mage was filled with a wild elation. It was hard for him to describe, but something was happening. He was *doing* something instead of just thinking, wondering and planning. It brought a gleam and glint of excitement to his eyes.

He came to a careening halt outside the brightly lit entrance of the ayuntamiento – the town hall, of which the police commissariat was but a part. Immediately figures crowded round the vehicle, among them Jaime Gomez with flattened hair and black serge uniform. As he swung open the passenger door, Hector hauled himself up onto the bench seat next to Mage, followed by a small man with rain slicked hair and sodden wet clothes. Mage only had the briefest of glimpses in the opaque light, but it was enough to see the ashen panic in the little man's eyes.

'Colin, there is no need for you to...'

'I'm driving! You navigate and direct!' Mage had already let out the clutch and the Land Rover was moving rapidly up the hill.

'Very well. I won't argue. Take the road to the Hozgarganta where you met me this morning...'

My God was it only that morning?

'... then take the mountain road up to the telegraph relay station. You were there, yes?'

'Yes.' Mage had a flash vision of the relay station and also of the single isolated farm house further down the other side of the mountain. He was suddenly certain that this was to be their ultimate destination.

'When the road ends there is a cart track that cuts across country down to Manolo's place. It's about another five kilometres on and the track will be bad: the rain has been heavy. Colin, again my thanks! I would never have got through in the Renault, even if she had been on the road.'

'Did Manolo walk all that way?' Mage asked, almost shouting above the engine noise which had risen dramatically now that they were driving along a short straight and he was able to pick up some real speed.

'Yes. As I say, it took him more than six hours.'

'What exactly is the problem with his wife?'

'She's gone into premature labour with her fourth child. She's a full month early. From the sound of it there are some nasty complications. If Manolo is right, she haemorrhaging badly and she's in great pain. I'll not be sure till I get there, but it does sound as if the baby is breached, and if that's the case I'm probably going to have to do a caesarean.'

'Don't you need a hospital for that sort of thing?'

'Colin, this is Campo Spain! The nearest hospitals are in La Linea or Algerciras! Campo women have been breach birthing since the beginning of history without the benefit of hospitals. True, it's a messy business and the mortality rate is high, but that's the way it is in this part of the world. We may have joined the EC and given up many of our old ways, but that's Cosmopolitan Spain, the Spain of the cities and the costas. This is The Campo, and Colin, although the rest of the nation may be racing to catch up with Europe, it's still like a third world country out here in the backlands. Normally, with a little luck, we'd probably be all right with what I've got here,' he patted the brown leather case that he hugged to his chest as it balanced and bounced on his knee, 'But on this particular occasion I must confess to being a little worried, which is why we're speaking English, by the way. I examined Dolores only last week and she seemed well enough then. Her other three children popped out as easily as peas from a pod. I'm hoping that our friend here is exaggerating somewhat. It's an Andalucian tendency after all. If he isn't, then I must tell you, I'm not looking forward to what is ahead. It will be a bloody night's work.'

The Land Rover hurtled across the iron bridge, at one point hitting a pothole and bouncing boneshakingly into the air. Mage was driving at no more than twenty five miles an hour but in the high seated vehicle with the visibility so dangerously restricted by the onslaught of the storm, it seemed much faster. Once on the hairpin mountain road he dropped the speed to under twenty in deference to the gradient but even this seemed too fast as Mage flung the car into the tight curves of the looping bends, using the four wheel drive to its maximum advantage.

'Colin, watch out for fallen trees and rocks. Even in a few hours, a storm like this can cause havoc.'

As if to confirm Hector's words a solid wall of water crashed across the bonnet and roof, and for a long second visibility was down to zero. Mage realised that they'd forded a small stream and the water falling down on them was only that which their passage had first thrown upwards. The Land Rover missed a beat and the ignition light flickered red until he built up the revs. There had been no stream crossing the road that morning and, duly sobered, Mage dropped into a lower gear, allowing their speed to decrease even more. It made for marginally easier handling, causing fewer bumps and enabling Mage to take a lighter grip on the madly bucking wheel, but the little Spaniard, sitting hunched and cramped in the corner, began to fret.

'Señor, can we go no faster? The children are alone, and Dolores, she...'

'Patience Manolo,' Hector soothed. 'It is a bad road and the English does well. It is better to get there a little late than not to get there at all. A few minutes will not make that much difference.'

I hope, thought Hector, full well knowing that in situations such as this more seconds could make the difference between a patient's life and death... And another thought came unbidden, one that had been lurking malignantly at the back of his mind ever since Jaime Gomez had phoned from the police commissariat. *What if this one is like the others?* His eyes hardened. *Well, if it is* – he thought of the extra hypodermic syringe he'd put into his bag before leaving Calle Santana, *if it is, then this time I know what I must do.*

A light flared. It was Colin, expertly lighting a cigarette with one hand, the Marlboro gripped firmly between his teeth. Good god, Hector thought, I really do believe that he's enjoying this! Yes, well I hope he continues to do so, and if he's going to come inside when we get to Manolo's I hope he has a strong stomach! This was not a night to be "enjoyed" but an emergency with a definite death risk, and yet – Hector's momentary resentment sparked and died as quickly as it had been born – and yet, when he'd needed the favour the Englishman had not hesitated and was this not the same man who had stopped that morning without being hailed down and asked, never forget, and had pulled Hector's car out of the gravel? The same man who, again without being asked, had towed Hector into the garage, saving him not one but two bills from the avaricious little mechanic.

Hector watched him now: the cigarette jutting defiantly from his lips, the black hat pulled down firmly, brim low across his forehead. His hands were a blur of movement on the steering wheel and the gear lever as he guided the lumbering vehicle around the steep hairpins. Hector would have been willing to drive himself if he'd had to, but was nonetheless glad that it was Mage who sat behind the wheel on this bloody awful night.

The branch of a tree cracked against the side of the cab. The Land Rover swerved, hit a deep rut, then bounced out again. Hector's head banged against the roof and he grabbed at the dashboard to steady himself.

'Sorry,' Mage grinned.

He is a strange one, Hector thought, and he *is* enjoying himself. Even stranger was the way that Anna had warmed to him. Despite her aversion to strangers, she'd been more animated and alive in Mage's company than Hector had ever seen her since the discovery of the glaucomas the previous year. Well that made Colin Mage all right in Hector's book. Anything, or anyone, who could bring Anna out of herself was once, twice and three times welcome.

'We're at the end of the road,' Mage shouted, hitting the brakes. 'The relay station's up there on the left. Which way from here?'

'Keep going straight on. Can you see the track?'

'Just about.' Mage leaned forward and peered through the almost opaque glass. He could barely discern the path they had to take. It was mostly pooled with water and visibility was less than ten feet. 'How well do you, or does he, know the road? I mean, can you talk me through it?'

Unthinkingly Mage had automatically spoken in Spanish. Manolo, even more agitated than before, responded immediately.

'A straight slope downwards for about thirty metres, then a sharp right curve followed by a longer left bend, with a much steeper down hill slope...'

'Got it,' Mage said, and pushing the gear selector into low ratio, eased the Land Rover forwards... The machine lurched sickeningly as the wheels went into soft mud and Mage concentrated on keeping the wheels moving. To stop now would be disastrous.

If Hector had asked, Mage would have owned up to the fact that this was the first time he'd tested the four wheel drive in really adverse conditions... That he was relatively new to the concept of off road driving! The Land Rover had been bought only a few weeks previously, half on intuitive impulse, half out of common sense, specifically with this trip to Spain in mind. Mage's low slung classic sports car would never have coped with Spain's rough roads, and the right deal had presented itself at the right time.

He'd been in the TVR, driving back into York after his second meeting with Michael Fry. As he'd turned the last corner into his street, an elegant tree lined avenue in one of the city's nicer districts, the garage on the corner had been moving the Land Rover out onto the forecourt. Mage had backed up and parked, attracted by the 'Rover's clean condition and solid chunky lines.

Rick Jackson, the proprietor, had sidled over. He and Mage had known each other for years and Mage also knew the Rick had long coveted the crimson Tuscan, now cooling at the curb.

'What's this Colin? Thinking of getting into FWD are we?'

'What's FWD?'

'Four Wheel Drive. The biggest selling new old idea since diesel.'

'This runs on diesel?'

'Nah. This is the petrol version. Fuel economy ain't so hot. You're only gonna get eighteen or twenty to the gallon and only then if you're driving her gently, but it's a lot quieter than a diesel, and a lot faster, a damn sight cheaper to put right if owt goes wrong. Not that it will,' he added hastily. 'This un's a good 'un. Fifteen years old, but only a genuine forty thou' on the clock and with a full service history to prove it. She's taxed and tested and comes with a no quibble six month guarantee.'

'How much?'

'To you Col, 'cos you're an old mate, a straight two and a half grand!'

Mage had walked around the Land Rover. The RAF blue paint work was without chip or flaw and the interior was nicely valeted in a plasticky utilitarian way.

'Really nice condition,' Rick had pressurised. 'Built of aluminium so they don't rust like ordinary motors. You can go through floods an' 'urricains in sommat like this...'

Mage had paused by the driver's door, one hand resting on the handle. A sudden precognitive image flashed across his mind of a stormy night, the Land Rover bucking, a sense of tension and excitement...

'All right Rick, you've talked yourself into it. Go and fetch your cheque book.'

'Me cheque book?'

Mage had nodded. 'If I've just bought your Land Rover for two and a half thousand pounds, you owe me about a thousand pounds because you've just bought my TVR.'

They'd haggled, but Mage had still walked away with the blue Land Rover and a cheque for nine hundred pounds. Now, less than six weeks later, the flash of clairvoyance was being proven accurate and the Land Rover was being put to the test and proving its worth with every yard travelled.

'A big rock and a sharp bend that goes left and very quick down at the same time!'

'Got it,' Mage yelled again, nearly hitting the rock and side sliding down the steep incline. The rain did not abate and jagged forks of lightening continued to dart and stab across the heavens. The cab of the Land Rover was damp and chill. His feet were wet and there was a prevalent smell of rubber and hot oil, but Hector was right! Despite the fear of risk, maybe even because of it, Mage was enjoying this Valkyrian ride through the night. He felt totally alive and charged with energy and he briefly wondered if Rick Jackson had kept the TVR or had sold it on.

They careened around one last treacherous bend and emerged into a waterlogged grove of eucalyptus trees. Over to the left was a low slung adobe bungalow with cracked walls and a broken porch. A dull orange glow shone dimly through filthy uncurtained windows.

'We are here,' Manolo shouted and immediately jumped out of the truck and half ran, half stumbled towards the house. Mage swung open the driver's door but felt Hector's restraining hand on his arm.

'Colin, there is no need for you to come inside. Wait for me here.'

'No, I'll come. Maybe I can help.'

'My friend, you have no medical skill – and it will not be very pleasant in there.'

'Hector, we're wasting time. Let's go.'

Mage jumped from the cab and sank to his ankles in freezing cold rainwater. Hurrying round the Land Rover he followed Hector into the house and walked straight into an earlier century.

The room was lit by candles and oil lanterns. An open fire flicked dolefully in one corner beneath a substantial black cauldron. The walls were adobe white and grey plaster and in most places the plaster was peeling. There was sawdust strewn across the floor and bundles of hay stacked haphazardly against the far wall. Three hens and a small dog clucked and yelped and had free run of the room. The furniture was obviously home made and rough hewn. Sitting at a table were two grubby and wide eyed girls, no more than four or five years old; a third child, little more than a babe, lay equally wide eyed in a cot, nervously pulling at something that had once been a doll.

To the left of the fire and in that part of the room that had the most light, there was an ancient iron bed, and writhing on the bed was the swollen and blood covered body of Manolo's wife, Dolores. Along with darkly oozing pools of crimson, she lay in her own ordure and frantically clutched at the head bars of the bed frame with whitened knuckles. The stench of filth and excreta was gagging and the sounds of her hoarse shrieks and moans was nothing less than pitiful.

Mage stood transfixed, but Hector moved forwards muttering 'Holy Mother of God' beneath his breath.

And then, 'Manolo, get the children out of here. Put them in the barn or in Colin's Land Rover and then come back and help me find some hot water.'

'There is hot water in the pot Señor. I filled it before I left and Sophia should have been topping it up.' Manolo crossed in front of Mage, moving towards the children. He glanced at the cauldron as he passed. 'Yes, there is much hot water. More than thirty litres.' Then he gathered up his children.

'Colin,' Hector snapped. 'Don't just stand there. Drag that cauldron over to the bed and let's get her cleaned up a bit. I can't see what I'm doing amid all this carnage.'

Mage broke out of his momentary fugue and, not without some effort, hauled the heavy black cauldron from the hearth, half carrying, half dragging it across the littered floor towards the end of the bed. Hector immediately scooped it up in handfuls and splashed it vigorously over Dolores' body, then, towelling her off with a less than clean piece of sheet, he began his examination, deftly and gently moving his hands across the grossly distended belly.

To Mage's eyes, the woman's skin seemed to crawl and ripple, as though there was something trapped inside her stomach that was determined to get out and escape any way it could. He suppressed a shiver and contained his feelings.

Snapping on a pair of rubber gloves and ignoring the woman's cries, Hector leaned forwards and began a cursory internal. Dolores' screams became more shrill and after only a very few moments Hector pulled back. Discarding the bloody gloves, he reached over to his bag and took out syringe. 'This is impossible! Let's see if we can get her on her side. I'm going to have to give her an epidural...'

But the woman, never less than eighteen stones since the birth of her first child and now deliriously crippled with pain, was not to be moved. Even with Manolo's help, the combination of dead-weight, angle of bed and the risk of inflicting unknown damage, defeated them. In the end, Hector exchanged syringes and injected into her wrist.

'It will quieten her down a bit, but not as much as I'd like. At least I'll be able to do the internal properly...'

Her screams diminished, although not by much. Hector produced new gloves and eased his way in. Mage watched, both fascinated and sickened as first Hector's fingers, and then his whole hand disappeared within the swollen and still bleeding vagina. After what seemed to be an eternity of tension, Hector finally groaned and withdrew his hand. Consigning the gloves to the fire, he tiredly took off his overcoat, paused for a moment, then turned and took Manolo's arm, looking him firmly in the eyes.

'I hate to do this to you my friend, but if it comes to it and I think it might, then who am I to save? The mother or the child?'

Manolo blanched. 'Doctor that is no decision to give me! How in the names of Jesus and Mary am I to make this choice?'

'I'm sorry Manolo, but choose you must – and there is precious little time for deliberation.'

Tears streamed down the little Spaniard's swarthy cheeks. 'Doctor Hector, give me at least one minute, one half minute with this...' He turned away, sobbing silently, head bowed.

'Is is really that bad?' Mage asked quietly in English.

'It's worse,' Hector looked at him strickenly. 'I cannot guarantee to save either life. If I do nothing, certainly both will die. If I can cut, then maybe and only maybe I can save one or the other. The child is breached but part of it is already jammed in the birth canal. I have to do a caesarean section and I have to do it as swiftly as I can to save the child. I can work just a little more slowly if I am to save the mother but that still means cutting the baby free and, either way, without a proper anaesthetic the shock to her system is going to be enormous and...'

Manolo touched Hector's shoulder, stifling his emotion and fighting for control. 'Señor Doctor,' he spoke formally, pulling himself up to his full height and full of gypsy pride. 'I know that you will do all that you can. I know that you will do your best. But if this choice must be made... Señor, I have three fine children but only one wife. Please, you must work for Dolores.'

'Very well. Now, go to your children. There is nothing you can do here. Give you little ones what comfort you can and do a little praying for us all, eh Manolo!'

Manolo nodded then quietly left.

'Damn,' Hector swore sadly and yet dispassionately. 'I wish I could save them both... But at least, thank God, he's given me the easier task.'

Again he showered her body with warm water, then drying his hands, pulled on a third pair of surgical gloves and produced a variety of syringes and scalpels. 'There'll be no cosmetic bikini line on this one,' he said gruffly.

' Hector – ' an odd tone in Mage's voice made the doctor look up. 'Would it help if she was deeply asleep and could feel no pain?'

'That would be the miracle of modern medicine, the wonder of a nice clean hospital delivery room with all the latest drugs. Regrettably we have no such facilities here.'

'But would it help?' Mage insisted. 'If she was deeply asleep and could feel no pain, would that help you save both mother and child?'

'In those circumstances I could virtually guarantee it, but...'

Mage was moving to the head of the bed. 'Then give me two minutes, Hector. Just two minutes. I'll tell you when you can start cutting.'

'But what are you going...'

Mage turned and just for a fleeting second, to Hector's eyes he no longer looked like the Englishman with whom he'd spent the better part of that day. For the space of one heart beat, he looked somehow taller and there was something of a different colour in his eyes.

'Trust me, Tio Palyasso, and I'll give you your anaesthetic.'

Something warm and unearthly exploded gently in Hector's solar plexus. *Tio Palyasso!* How had Mage known that name. None had called him Tio Palyasso for twenty three years and even then it was a unique name that Mariana had thought up for him when she'd wanted to tease. *How did the English have this name?* Not even Anna Maria knew of it, so how could Mage know?

Hector opened his mouth to speak, but Mage had turned his back on him and was now sitting on the edge of the bed near the sweaty and vomit stained pillow.

'I'll tell you when to cut...' It was Mage's voice and yet it *wasn't*! 'Be ready, and once you start, keep me informed as to how you're progressing.'

***

'Yeva vishua, yeva yeahod, sooshi kosh quandosii...' Mage chanted the mantra over and over again, never varying the pitch or phonetic emphasis. Leaning over the woman he massaged her temples with the first and second fingers of each hand. His thumbs held her eyelids open and holding his face close to hers, forced her to focus on his eyes. At first her pupils darted all over the place, not seeing him – but then as her screams diminished to moans and whimpers, eye contact was made. For a second there was blind panic as she tried to close her eyes and couldn't, then her eyes defocused completely and rolled backwards into her head. The whimpering fell away into a silence that seamed deafening. Outside the rain crashed against the leaves of the forest and the tin roof of the nearby barn counterpointed by the buffeting wind and distant thunder. The fire crackled in a desultory way, there was a steady drip of water leaking from the roof, splashing with regular monotony against the stained metal of the sink. Dolores' breathing became deep and regular.

Mage ceased the softly chanted mantra and removed his thumbs from the eyelids which immediately closed shut. Maintaining the gentle pressure against her temples with his finger tips, he called quietly over his shoulder.

'All right Hector. You can start.'

'I do not believe this!'

'Start cutting Hector, but take your time. There's no rush now. I can hold her like this for as long as you want. She will feel nothing.'

With one part of his mind in a daze – he would not have believed this possible had he not seen it for himself – Hector picked up the tools of his trade and went to work. He cut deeply into the abdomen from just below the navel right down to the pubis. Dolores made no sound and nor did she flinch as Hector's scalpel cut into her. She simply carried on breathing regularly as if in a deep and dreamless sleep.

Hector freed the embryo from the womb and birth canal and lifted it from the body. He looked at it only once, feeling a coldness clutch at his heart and bowels. Bile and vomit rose in his throat. Laying the body on the floor and ignoring its tiny bleats of life, he swiftly took a hypodermic needle from the secondary pocket of his bag and, kneeling on the dark tiles, injected the contents of the syringe directly into the baby's chest. It died immediately and he covered it with one of the discarded sheets. He then went back to work on Dolores, stitching, suturing and steadily closing the gaping caesarean wound.

'How are you doing?' asked Mage, not turning from the head of the bed.

Hector was silent for a second. 'I'm closing her up now. How long can you keep her like this?'

'How long do you want her to sleep for?'

'Twenty four hours?' Hector laughed coldly. 'Can you do that?'

'Yes, if necessary, but I'll have to let her sleep naturally, so if you're serious about twenty four hours it means I'll have to sit here for twenty four hours, taking her down again every time she starts to regain consciousness.'

'All right. Just hold her until I'm finished here then I'll give her a couple of jabs, one for the body shock and one to keep her knocked out for half a day. At least, I can do that now...'

'Hector - the baby?'

'Stillborn.' There was ice in the doctor's voice and beads of perspiration on his brow.

In the light of the rain swept dawn, dark grey clouds scudded across a washed out sky. Instinctively, Mage pulled the Land Rover off the road and the two men sat silently surveying the village, drenched and dim in the dawnlight, half a mile away.

Mage brought out a crumpled pack of cigarettes, took one then passed the packet to Hector. The doctor unthinkingly helped himself then tossed the packet onto the dashboard and reached for his matches. They were wet and would not light. Mage passed over the brass zippo.

Hector inhaled the smoke deeply, then turned to look at his companion. There was a calmness in the Englishman that simply had not been there before... But there was also challenge. Mage met his eyes and in the end it was Hector who finally looked away.

'What did you do back there, Colin?'

'What do you think I did, Hector?'

'I don't know.' The doctor, tired beyond belief and battling with conscience and the Hippocratic oath, looked up from the cigarette. 'Some kind of hypnotism? Let me tell you, my friend, that I know something about hypnotism and I have even practised it on occasion, but never in all my life have I seen anything like what you did to Dolores... And,' he hesitated, 'how did you know about Tio Palyasso? Answer me that, my new English friend, for if you can't, then our friendship can travel no further than this night.'

'It was mostly hypnotism,' Mage conceded carefully, 'but please don't worry about it and please don't ask too many questions because it's impossible to give you all of the answers. I have certain – talents and it's difficult to explain how they work, even to myself. I have a psychic gift. It enables me to see things and know things about people that I have no right to know. It doesn't control me, but then, nor can I always control it. Sometimes the gift isn't a gift at all, but a curse, and I have to work very hard on occasion to ignore what my senses are telling me. That isn't always possible and I find that I've done something or said something before I've had time to think about it. So it was with Tio Palyasso... I know that it means Uncle Clown, but I don't exactly know what it means to you. Things were getting very tense back there and I knew that I had to get your attention... I knew that I had to make you trust me and Tio Palyasso just popped out of its own accord. I'm sorry if I worried you, but at least we can be thankful that my gift was put to some good use.'

Hector sighed and closed his eyes. 'I've heard about people like you, but you're the first one I've actually met.' He smiled mirthlessly. 'I would welcome the opportunity of talking to you some more on the subject, but while you are in this part of Spain it may be to your advantage to keep your gifts to yourself. The people here are superstitious. They would soon start calling you El Bruho...'

'I'm not a witch, Hector.'

'No of course you're not but that's what people would call you anyway. And I am thankful for your help tonight, for without it I'd have lost both child and mother...'

In his mind's eye, Hector remembered walking into the forest, bundle under one arm, spade resting in the crook of the other. He'd sweated, digging deep in the soft wet soil for more than half an hour, before depositing the bundle at the bottom of the grave, then filling in the hole, covering the loose surface earth with large stones and small rocks. Afterwards, he'd had to tell Manolo what he'd done, a defiant Manolo who'd insisted that the baby be given a proper burial in the village until Hector had whispered furiously in his ear.

'Manolo, the priests would never bury it. The baby was wrong, very wrong. That's what nearly killed Dolores! Do you understand, Manolo? The baby was wrong!'

Comprehension of what Hector was saying came slowly to the campero's face, but when it finally did arrive, he'd nodded silently, gripping the doctor's hand in mute gratitude. How much better to say that the baby had been stillborn and had been buried with prayers and dignity on his own land than to risk the pointing fingers and wagging tongues of the village. There had been too many tales of wrong babies over the last few seasons. Far better he be thought of as a miserly peon than the carrier of bad seed.

'What was wrong with the baby?' Mage's words cut through Hector's reverie like razor blades.

'What makes you ask such a question?' The doctor asked indignantly. 'I told you. It was stillborn.'

'If you say so then I shall believe you,' Mage spoke softly, 'but as I said, I have certain talents and I felt there was more to it than that. If we are to be friends, Hector Sanchez, let us remember that truth is a two way thing. If the baby was only stillborn, why haven't we brought it with us to be buried in Castillo? I know enough of Spanish customs to understand this would be the normal thing for us to do.' And then, as Hector felt the younger man's eyes boring into him... 'There *was* something wrong with it, wasn't there?'

The doctor looked out of the window, absently wiping at the condensation with a grubby sleeve. Two hundred metres away, the Rio Hozgarganta churned beneath the iron bridge; its waters, brackish brown, were filled with debris – branches of trees, the corpse of a goat. He shivered in the damp of his clothes and fumbled for his pipe. This was a futile gesture for the old briar was jammed with wet tobacco and would need a thorough decoking before it would smoke again properly. Nonetheless, the took some comfort from holding the familiar oval shape in the palm of his hand.

'The child was deformed.' He spoke in a low voice, slowly and pedantically. 'Badly so...' He blinked his eyes and saw again the monster that he'd taken from Dolores' distended body. The head was twice as big as it should have been and the arms and feet had been stunted and claw like. The scales on the thing's body had been the most repulsive element. The scales and the eyes, eyes which had been green slits of malevolence that had watched with dispassionate intelligence even as Hector had injected the massive killing dose of pentothal. What would have been the outcome of allowing the thing to live? And there was no doubt in Hector's mind that the thing would have lived and thrived unless Dolores had quietly smothered it or until Manolo had hit it with an axe in the solitude of the forest.

There would have been the speculations, investigations and accusations, just as there had been before, and look at what that had led to! In one case divorce, in another murder and in a third case suicide and madness. Simple ordinary lives turned upside down and thrown into an abyss of pain and confusion, and born of what? Certainly not superstition for there was nothing of fantasy or imagination in the physical reality of the dozen or so deformed creatures that he had seen in the past months. So *what* then?

Something in the water? No, he'd checked and double checked. Something in the food chain? No, because he'd checked and double checked that as well. Something in the air? A spore or gene or virus, possibly drifting over from the big American base at Rota or from the nuclear stockpile in Gibraltar? In the best traditions of investigative medicine, Hector had been most thorough in his checking, analysing both the water supply and the food chain and also the quality of the air. He'd found nothing.

Then he'd made very discreet phone calls and learned that nowhere else was affected. Only Castillo and the Castillato Valley was producing this pattern of premature births, some stillborn, all badly misshapen and mutated. And those few that had lived had only lived for a few hours until some fatal domestic accident befell them, leaving the inevitable aftershock of guilt and accusation.

Few knew the true figures, although most were aware of one or two occurrences. As the area's only doctor, Hector knew exactly how many times it had happened and the numbers frightened him.

'How many times?' Mage asked, and Hector's eyes narrowed. What was this? Was the Englishman reading his mind even as his thoughts were forming?

'Thirteen times in eighteen months. Three times this year alone since January.'

Colin Mage sat and thought furiously about what Hector had told him. The implications were very relevant to Mage's purpose for being in Castillo and although he couldn't tie in all the data, he was certain there was a link somewhere.

'What about the birth rate in general?' he finally asked.

Hector shrugged. 'It's above normal, about twelve or fifteen percent, but the harvests have been good for the last two years and the people have been happier and more relaxed, and with more money in their pockets. That could easily account for it...' Hector trailed into silence, the great ball of grief moving up from his solar plexus to his throat, threatening to choke him. His load was a heavy one and he'd carried it too long alone. Tentatively, he reached out for Mage's arm... When he spoke again, it was barely more than a whisper. His was a soul in search of absolution.

'Listen Colin, I gave Dolores' baby an injection. I put it to sleep. For the sake of the family. For the sake of this village and its people. I have played God and will answer to the angels for it with a broken oath. I tell you this because my heart is aching for what happened back there and for what seems to be happening in our Valley.' And then, 'I needed to tell someone. I have been tempted to do this thing many times and always before I have drawn back. But last night... Last night was too much and I had to do something.'

Mage rested his hand lightly on the doctor's shoulder. 'You don't have to explain it. I do understand.'

'Do you? How can you?'

'I understand very clearly...' Mage paused, thinking and making a decision. 'Hector, I never really knew my parents and I was more or less brought up by my grandmother. She was an incredible woman, as tough as old boot leather. We were very close and it was always an intense and unusual relationship. She was mother, father, teacher and friend, all rolled into one.

'She never had a day's serious illness in her life and she never lost her wits or determination to live life on anything but her own terms. I can remember her painting and decorating the house one year...' Mage chuckled quietly. 'She was up and down ladders like a yo yo, slapping on paint and papering walls and she was in her late eighties even then!

'Anyway, sooner or later it had to happen and one day she felt poorly. The next day she was in hospital with pulmonary pneumonia. She came home a couple of weeks later, but the spark had gone out of her. She was well over ninety and she'd started to die.

'After a few weeks it got so that she didn't bother getting out of bed any more and most days she was asleep more often than she was awake. But it was a painful process and she loathed it. She'd lost the energy to live, but not the will.

'There wasn't anybody else. Only me. Towards the end I had to do everything for her – you know, from spoon feeding to changing the bedclothes, the dirty linen – everything. She couldn't even use the lavatory without me being there to hold her in place. Then she became incontinent and it didn't really matter any more, although it made my work load ten times heavier and it was a grave offence against her dignity. She was in permanent pain and discomfort, but nothing hurt her more than her loss of independence and the even greater loss of her pride. She simply couldn't cope with the helplessness...

'The social people wanted to put her into a home, but the thought terrified her and I can't say that it appealed to me much either. We both knew that once in, she'd never be coming out again and we both fought bitterly against that truth.

'Towards the end it got so bad that she begged me to end it for her. I knew that I *couldn't* and when I mentioned it, very carefully I might add, to our attending doctor, he made it perfectly clear that he *wouldn't*...'

'Anyway, this particular night, she was moaning and whimpering. She'd been bed bound for fourteen weeks and the bed sores were all over her frail old body by then. I was exhausted and couldn't sleep – God, I hadn't slept properly for weeks – and in the end, when she eventually fell quiet for a while, I finally found the courage to do what she'd been asking me to do for ages.

'I took a pillow from my bed and walked down the hall to her room. I tell you, Hector, I felt awful. I was crying and hurting, but I knew I couldn't let her go on suffering. In the end I went in and I was just about to cover her face with the pillow when something, I'm not sure what, made me wait a second. And then a shaft of moonlight came in through the window and rested on her face.

'She was calm and serene, looking like the old lady she'd been at seventy. She seemed to be sleeping, but...'

'She'd already gone?' Hector asked quietly.

'Yes, she'd already gone... But if she hadn't, I know I would have done it. I'd not have let her go on with any more of the awful suffering she was going through. Looking back now, I just wish I'd found the courage to do it many weeks earlier. But the point of all this is to let you know that I do know how you feel and you'll have no criticism from me...' And then as a deliberate afterthought... 'And no breach of confidence either!'

'Thank you, Colin. Thank you.'

'Tell me about Anna. What's the matter with her eyes?'

Hector looked up, momentarily startled by the sudden shift in conversation. Then, the tiredness and overloading emotions taking over, he visibly relaxed. After all, this was the Englishman who could defy the laws of medicine, the Englishman who had known that he was a doctor even before he had been informed of the fact. This was the Englishman who knew what you were thinking even as you thought it. The Englishman who could read minds. Why then, should he be surprised if he knew about Anna?'

'Anna has a brain tumour,' Hector said bleakly. 'She is going blind. She will be without sight before the end of the year... and unless some miracle happens to arrest the tumour's growth, she'll probably be dead by the end of next year. She knows about the blindness, but she doesn't know the rest. Now you know. God knows why I've told you, but I have done and I charge you not to breathe this information to another living soul...'

Hector rubbed at the misty windscreen with the back of his hand and peered out into the growing light. 'I have lived in the village for fourteen years and it has been a good place to live. But now something is changing. Something is going wrong... The people are changing and the changes are too sudden to be natural. We have rich harvests, but badly deformed babies... And it isn't just the children either. Some of the things that are falling from the bellies of our sheep and cattle come straight from the bowels of hell! People are becoming frightened and aggressive; we have murders and suicides and cases of insanity... Things which would have been unheard of in a place like this a couple of years ago. The whole atmosphere, the ambience... Seems to have fallen down the face of the cliff.'

He turned and looked enigmatically at Mage. 'I'll tell you something now which is funny, but I don't think it will make you laugh much. I am a man of medicine, if you like, a man of science. I am not given to flights of fancy or the wild imaginings of a village washer woman, and yet I look out of your Land Rover's window upon the village that has been my home for all these years, and do you know what I feel? I'll tell you what I feel! I feel frightened. Something very strange and wrong has come to dwell among us in Castillo de la Frontera. Now, my very clever Englishman, tell me you think I'm mad, eh?'

'No Hector,' Mage stubbed out his cigarette and turned on the ignition. 'I don't think you're mad. I think you're right. There is something wrong in Castillo...' He shot Hector a look that Hector would not easily forget. '... And that, Doctor Sanchez, is why I'm here.'

The adventure continues in 'The Opening' available now from Humdrumming.

An excerpt from...

THE IMAGINEER
BY GREGORY ASHE

ISBN 1-905532-00-8 - SNOWSCAPE EDITION
ISBN 1-905532-01-6 - FIRE EYE EDITION

"If it were that easy, we'd all be heroes"

This is not it. The world you know - normal, safe, boring - is just a stepping stone to other worlds, other places. Places of magic, monsters and limitless imagination.

Like most eleven year olds, Charlie Whittaker always hoped this was true.
Now he *knows* it is.
Because somebody's kidnapped his Uncle and he's forced to give chase.

Leaving normality far behind...

He will make friends on the way: the enigmatic Lashram, the absurd Squintillion, the noble Algernon. He will see sights that will make the wildest dreams of his life seem bland.

But will he survive long enough to enjoy them? There are horrors out there, ravenous cannibals, lethal assassins and, of course The High Lord Jethryk – a man who wears shadows torn from his victims and could snuff out all life in the universe using no more than his smooth fingertips. There is, in fact, only one power Jethryk doesn't possess, a power he intends to steal from Charlie's uncle.

By whatever means necessary.

It's all about story you see, and the power of imagination, one false word and creation as we know it will cease to exist...

The Imagineer is a beautifully illustrated novel that hearkens back to the child in all of us, a modern fairytale that will excite older children and adults alike. There are other worlds to explore: sometimes wonderful, sometimes terrifying, always spectacular.

All you have to do is believe...

Once upon a time, when the world had barely learned to walk, the people lived in a settlement to the north. They were a simple folk, with little to call their own. They lived in huts that they made using the wood from the trees and the mud that sits at the river's bottom. They hunted what they ate and the skins of the animals that lined their stomachs also lined their backs. They had nothing and wanted less.

But as the years fell by, some of them began to feel empty; they felt a yearning that they hadn't the words to name. Something was missing from their lives but they didn't know what.

They elected leaders from the wise men and set them to task; the wise men must discover what it was that they lacked, and once discovering it, *provide* it.

And so the wise men set to work. For years they cogitated and ruminated, ummed and aahed, until eventually they decided the best course of action. A strong, young, man should be chosen to leave the settlement and search the world outside for an answer. The people were impressed with this (despite the fact that the wise men, like most wise men, had in fact thought of nothing).

One of their number was chosen to go, he was given food to eat and water to drink. In his hand they placed a spear so that he could protect himself from the monsters that surely dwelt outside the borders of their land. With many fond farewells and words of encouragement the young man set off on his quest.

The days passed by in the settlement, then the months and then the years. The wise men that had devised the plan grew old and died to be replaced by others and then others still. Soon the quest was all but forgotten, nothing but vague memories passed down from parent to child.

It was then that the man returned, as young as the day he had left (for he had lived life too fast for age to catch him). Their memories awakened, the people gathered 'round full of questions. Quietly, he silenced them and bid them sit down.

He told them a story. They sat down and listened, in awe of the magic from beyond their land. When he had finished, they laughed, cried and begged him for another and another and another and... Still they wanted more.

The sun grew high in the sky and The Storyteller grew hot, so he planted a tree to give him shade and sat underneath it while it grew. As it grew, so did his stories, its branches spread wider and wider, every leaf a story, every story a leaf.

The storyteller had sons; he cut a branch from the tree and divided it between them. He gave each of them a seed, so that they could walk the world, plant a tree and tell their own stories.

They walked far and wide; spreading the stories as their power grew stronger, until the stories became truth. And then they spoke the moon and the stars; they spoke the great lands to the East and the wide wide seas that would divide them.

Soon no one was empty, and the World became a story that was spoken out loud.

The adventure continues in 'The Imagineer' available now from Humdrumming with two alternate cover designs - the Snowscape Edition and the Fire Eye Edition.

A Christmas Carve-up
Steve Newman & Laurence Buxton

Coming soon to Humdrumming...

SWANN & PARKER: THE CRIME OF THE CRIMEA

By Steve Newman & Laurence Buxton - ISBN 1-905532-06-7

In 1882, when Henry Donaldson, one of Britain's most acclaimed actors, is murdered on the stage of the Memorial Theatre, Stratford-upon-Avon, during the first performance of The Crime of the Crimea, the rest of the cast, and several members of the public, find themselves under suspicion.

It is another case for the intrepid police duo of Detective Inspector Swann, and Detective Sergeant Parker, of the new Criminal Investigation Department of the County Police Force.

But nothing is at it seems. What secrets are being kept? And what lies told? And who will die next? And is everyone really who they say they are?

Can the old sleuth, and ex-soldier, DI Herbert Swann, and DS John Parker, unravel the dramatic twists and turns of this horrific, hilarious, sexy, and darkly gothic, murderous mystery?

Steve Newman & Laurence Buxton have created in Swann & Parker a 19th century detective double act that will live as long as crime fiction exists.

"Get that Ghost Of Christmas Past off the stage, Parker."

Chief Inspector Herbert Swann had given this bold order. It was December the 21st, 1878. An ice-cold wind blew tiny snowflakes hither and thither, and the packed ice on the ground was showing no signs of thawing.

Meanwhile, inside the still unfinished Shakespeare Memorial Theatre, Stratford-upon-Avon, the rotund, ruddy-faced and bewhiskered Swann was installing a sense of order, something that he'd always known how to do since seeing the British Army's best, and worst, efforts in the Crimea, in his youth.

"Get him off the *stage*, my good man!" he repeated.

Detective Sergeant Parker obeyed, and with the polite firmness he used but rarely, shooed the various members of the cast back down to where the audience would be – well, would *have* been – when the play opened in three days' time. A one-off performance of Charles Dickens' 'A Christmas Carol' on Christmas Eve had been the intention, to see how the new theatre responded to an audience so to speak. The show had understandably sold out.

But the performance had become a one-off in more ways than one, thought Swann wryly. The lead actor, Merrick Carver, had been acting his heart out in this evening's rehearsal, as Ebenezer Scrooge. He had been protesting, in character, that no apparition could force him to change his ways. He had stood in the usual place, saying the usual words, and could never have predicted what was to happen.

As the shambling, irascible Scrooge grew to a crescendo of indignant fury at the dire warnings made against him, he found himself suddenly descending at huge speed through the trapdoor in the stage. His walking stick had shot into the air, an involuntary act of surprise, and he had descended onto a series of particularly evil metal spikes, of the sort more commonly found upon gates. The result of this incident was not pretty.

Parker spoke at last.

"Awful way to go, sir."

Swann agreed without even looking round.

"Most awful, Parker. Most awful."

"You know, I always liked this play, sir. Won't look at it in quite the same way again."

Swann tutted.

"It appears the ghosts are becoming less tolerant of Mr. Scrooge. I seem to remember he was given a second chance."

Parker looked down the dark chasm of the trapdoor, where the unfortunate Carver had fallen.

"He wasn't given any chance at all, if you ask me, sir. Someone clearly knew what they were doing."

Swann concurred.

"Yes. It seems that somebody knew exactly where Mr. Carver would be standing, and when. Those spikes have obviously been put there for a grim purpose, and fastened so the falling body would be impaled fatally. Whoever did this wasn't taking any chances the poor man might simply break a leg or bruise an arm in the fall."

There came a five-minute hiatus, while other members of the local constabulary, including the ever reliable Constable Lewis, helped to haul the body from the pit into which it had so dramatically plummeted. Finally, it was laid down upon the stage, minus the false beard, which had been shaken off the late actor's chin by the movements of the winch and pulley system used to extract the body from the trap.

Parker checked the numerous holes in the body with a pathologist's expertise.

"Interesting wounds these, sir."

Swann looked at his second-in-command with curiosity.

"In what way?"

Parker continued:

"Well the length of the spikes used seems to be just enough to have caused terminal damage to the man's nervous system. No organs punctured, from what I can see. The death was caused from the shock of the impact."

Swann was intrigued.

"Ah yes! I saw similar things at Sebastopol. Now when the Russians had entrenched themselves in that hellish port, they had some rather nasty…"

He began a tale of his time in the Crimea. But Constable Lewis had his own concerns, as the hitherto patient cast began to complain about the way they were being treated. Like criminals, no less! Particularly vocal had been Sam Watson, a crusty old actor who played Bob Cratchett.

"I have a very important soiree to attend this evening," he announced loudly and repeatedly to anyone who would listen. He was being particularly troubled by the tousle-haired, freckled-faced young child actor who portrayed Tiny Tim, who kept yanking at his jacket, a filthy garment the actor had never much liked. Finally, the precocious young boy was given a hard slap on the side of the head by the curmudgeonly Watson knocking the aforesaid Tim into the middle of a metaphorical next week.

Swann looked less than impressed at this behaviour among the actors. On top of Sam's wish to attend a champagne buffet, especially with one of the cast – the lead member, no less – lying flat on his back, dead, upon the stage, the others - with the exception of the boy who was now staggering about in something of a daze - were getting a bit awkward, and restless too.

The three ghosts, of Christmas Past, Present and Future, were all eyeing up Mrs. Cratchett. But Past had done himself no favours when he had talked of his own fondness for a big bird, only for his reference to the enormous (and fake) turkey to be misconstrued by the actress, who had strayed within earshot. It was not exactly a secret that the actress in question verged on the Rubenesque, and was probably not the ideal member of the cast to convince an audience she was starving at yuletide. Nonetheless, the producer, a young, flippant fellow by the name of Compton, who was no fool, had deliberately staged her scenes so that she would always be wearing a shawl, and be placed behind a table or cooking pot. That would make the impoverished and underpaid Cratchetts seem more convincing.

Present believed he was doing quite well, but he always felt a little annoyed that his part, being sandwiched between the two more dramatic characters of his fellow 'apparitions', couldn't really impress the woman, whose carnal appetites were reportedly as wanton as her feeding ones. Yet his classical good looks, if a little pasty when his make-up was added, should eventually get the job done with the generously proportioned Miss Clodheart, who was currently eating a slice of goose pate, a pork pie, and half a loaf of bread washing the lot down with a couple of bottles of Flowers' India Pale Ale.

Future, however, was also wondering if the two of them – Miss Clodheart and himself - could *have* a future? Something that vexed him heartily. Though relatively young and inexperienced in matters of the opposite sex, Future knew he had to have, preferably sooner rather than later, Clodheart for his own. He sighed. At least the death of that rotten egg Carver might bring him a little closer to his goal, the sight of his broken and bleeding body at the bottom of the pit had not upset him in the least. Looking at the behaviour of the others, he clearly wasn't alone.

The same thought had occurred to Swann. He glanced at the tombstone prop that stood at the back of the stage. It was the sight of this, of course, that was the turning point for Scrooge in the play. But now it suddenly had an added significance. The lead actor had changed the course of fate – both for himself and for the unfortunate, unknowing Ebenezer. In a way both now lay dead upon the stage, in the shadow of the tombstone, their bodies convulsed and their faces contorted.

"So, Parker. This Merrick fellow…"

Parker pre-empted the question. "Bit grumpy by all accounts."

"Motive, Parker? Was there a motive for this 'accident'?"

"Well no sir. You see, he might not have been a… well… barrel of laughs *exactly*, but he wasn't a bad old soul either. As long as he had his brandy after a performance and a chariot ready to take him back to a nice warm hotel room, he was quite happy."

Swann was suddenly aware of Miss Clodheart glancing at him with an anxious look, only to break off this stare when realising her glance was being returned.

"And I think we can probably guess who was keeping it warm." A slow smile spread across most of Swann's apparently good-natured countenance. As they say in France, *cherchez la femme*. When a motive is hard to find, just *cherchez la femme*.

At that moment Constable Lewis returned from his duties dealing with the cast.

"Ah, Lewis!" called out Swann. "Found anything?"

"No, sir. But I think I've lost something!" The unmistakeable Swansea tones of the policeman couldn't hide his fluster.

" Lost something?"

"My watch. That soddin' Tiny bloody Tim, I reckon. If I find he's got it, sir, I'll be making his Christmas one he won't forget, and it won't be the turkey that gets stuffed, indeed it won't."

Swann smiled and moved over to Compton who was sat on the corner of the stage fretting at the hem of his jacket, counting lost box office pennies no doubt.

"Would I be right in thinking we're missing someone Mr. Compton?"

The producer looked perplexed for a moment, continuing to tug at his jacket, then he nodded.

"I presume you mean Marley's Ghost?"

"There is a distinct lack of rattling chains sir, yes."

Compton sighed and got to his feet.

"That was our first disaster Inspector, Roderick collapsed a couple of days ago, he's been convalescing ever since."

"I presume he's received medical attention?"

"Of course, the after effects of siege fatigue apparently. He was something of a hero in the Crimea I believe."

"Ah." Swann nodded and thought, as he often did, that he fancied he heard the sound of distant munitions fire. "A terrible thing sir, terrible. Tell me, what precisely are the symptoms?"

Compton chuckled, though there was little humour in it.

"Oh nothing less than partial paralysis! He's been in a wheelchair ever since, even needs help being fed I hear. I tell you, the Carver family don't like to do things by halves."

"The Carver family? Forgive me sir but I don't follow."

"Roderick, Roderick *Carver*, he was Merrick's brother." Compton sighed, "Dear God, just think what this news will do for his recovery."

"You mean to say nobody has told him?"

Compton shook his head. "What with everything else it just didn't occur to me."

Swann's moustache rippled irritably.

"Well sir, might I suggest that someone does so?" He turned to leave and then, with another thought, turned back. "Is Mr. Carver under medical supervision?"

"Yes, his doctor is an old friend from the war, I believe he's staying with him at the moment."

"Then would you be good enough to ask Mr. Carver to join us here?"
Compton looked shocked, a grimace of abject fear on his babyish features.
"Do you really think that's wise Inspector?"
Swann smiled.
"I think it's the least we should do sir, see to it would you?"

Parker was beginning to lose his patience with 'Theatrical Legend' Sam Watson. If the old ham outlined the deficiencies of the late Merrick Carver's performance as the lead any further he would order Lewis to give the man a gentle beating with his truncheon. Noticing the red faced Welshman, over Watson's shoulder, getting more and more exasperated by the baiting of 'Tiny Tim', it occurred to Parker that he just may do it too.
"The problem you see Inspector is a simple one. Carver simply had no stage presence, something no amount of direction or private study can provide."
Watson coughed falsely and brushed some non-existent fluff from the front of his silken waistcoat.
"For myself, I have always been blessed in that area. Why, my Claudius was said to rival the Dutch Prince himself. My Prospero had a magic all of its own, according to one insightful reviewer."
Parker clenched his fists even tighter behind his back.
"It must have been something of a disappointment then sir, what with such a glittering career behind you, to have been relegated to a mere supporting character in this production."
"Young man! I should have been playing Scrooge. Not that toss pot, Carver!"
The room fell silent at his shouting, all heads turning towards him.
Watson harrumphed and resumed the brushing of his waistcoat with his spindly fingers.
"Well… that's my opinion anyway."

Swann turned, and raised an eyebrow at Watson's outburst.
"He certainly has the vocal projection for the part," he muttered.
"The arrogance too."
Swann had taken to questioning the Ghost of Christmas Future and had already formed the opinion that he was a very bitter young man.
"I take it you don't, how shall we put it? See eye to eye with the noble Watson?"
The young man scoffed. "Who could with a head that far in the clouds?"
"Would that go for Mr. Carver too?"
"Oh no, that old goat had his feet on the ground Inspector." Swann noticed the brief glance the fellow gave to Mrs. Clodheart at that point, "Manipulative swine knew *exactly* what he was doing."
"Do I take it you are suggesting some form of impropriety on Carver's part regarding Mrs. Clodheart?" The young man gawped in shock. "Your feelings are rather obvious young man."
The Ghost sighed and nodded gently.
"Much good it may do me." He fixed Swann with a glare steelier than the Inspector had seen in men twice his age, "But yes… I am suggesting 'impropriety' on his part. The braggart had no feelings for her whatsoever, he was just using her for her…"
"Quite."
"Well… He was even seen arm in arm with a local woman strolling along Waterside as pretty as you please, flaunting his duplicity. I tried to tell her but…" The young man gazed down at his stockinged feet, "Well… she wouldn't listen."
Swann nodded. "Perhaps she did." He then noticed Parker making eye contact

with him from across the auditorium, made his excuses and moved over to him.

"So Parker, 'not a bad old soul' I think were your words."
Parker smiled and shrugged in embarrassment.
"I might want to revise that opinion."
"The night is yet young."
"They've brought Roderick Carver from his lodgings."
Swann glanced over at the bundle of blankets being wheeled in through the main door.
"So I see, I trust someone had the foresight not to leave his brother's corpse lying about?"
"All tidied away sir."
"Good, we've enough theatrical scenes here as it is." He flashed Parker a mischievous smile, "Enjoying the show so far?"
"Enlightening sir."
"Good, *good*, well, I suppose we'd better have a word with the family."
They walked over to Carver's side, nodding at the man stood beside him.
"Doctor?"
"Milverton, yes. I must say I'm rather displeased at the treatment my patient is receiving at your hands, Inspector. Roderick should be at home resting."
"It's alright Augustus," A weak voice came from within the woollen tartan in the wheelchair. "I want to help in any way that I can."
Swann was quick to respond.
"Thank you sir, your sense of duty is honourable. But then I would expect no less from a man with your service record."
"Thank you Inspector, but I assure you my primary motive is just to see whoever committed this atrocious crime hanging at the end of the rope." Carver's voice cracked and he held a small white handkerchief to his eyes.
"I quite understand sir. I'll try not to detain you long."
Swann stood up and moved to a quiet corner with Parker at his side.
"Well sir, I'm blowed if I know what to make of it all. Seems to me they could all have done it."
"Not quite my good fellow, we have established multiple motives certainly but there remains the matter of immutable fact."
"I don't follow."
"Watch and learn Parker, watch and learn,"
Swann then turned back to the cast.
"Ladies and Gentlemen, if I may have your indulgence for one further request. Would you all please adopt the precise positions you were in at the moment of the accident."

When everyone had assumed their positions, with a little jostling here and there, Detective Inspector Herbert Swann addressed them, and they hung on his every word. And Swann, while appreciating the irony, also appreciated the moment. As a lover of the arts, and contributor to the theatre, on the quiet, he loved the fact that here were the so-called professionals looking to him for guidance.
"Ladies and gentlemen this is a most bizarre case. A murder in the theatre. In front of all the cast! Not the make-believe death of the unloved Ebenezer Scrooge, but the very real death of Merrick Carver. A private man, a fine character actor – and, now, a very *dead* man."
He glanced at the faces ranged around him: the young boy - still looking a bit dazed - old Sam, the three ghosts, Miss Clodheart, they all looked stunned. Perhaps

finally the seriousness of the situation had settled into their muddled thespian brains? Miss Clodheart even seemed to have tear-stained cheeks. Was her resolve cracking, or was it the grease from the goose pate?

"I'm ashamed to admit," continued Swann, "that I went, like poor Mr. Carver, down a dead end. I naturally assumed that this case was all about a lady, young Mistress Clodheart there. That her obvious attractions were in themselves motive enough for murder." The lady in question suddenly roused herself. "But she is not the reason that the ill-fated Merrick lies dead tonight in Stratford mortuary. Though she clearly has quite an effect on the men in the cast, or rather, the *phantoms* in the cast." Past, Present and Future all looked at each other rather worriedly. "No, I soon came to the realisation that I was, as they say, barking up the wrong theatrical tree."

Swann caught himself strutting across the stage, raising one arm as if to proclaim, like Caesar. Dear Lord but he was rather enjoying this.

"No. There were many possible motives in this room but they add up to nothing once you appreciate one small detail."

Parker looked as bewildered as the cast.

"What do you mean, sir?"

Swann smiled at Parker.

"Well, Sergeant Parker." He smiled even more broadly. "John." Parker looked less than delighted at the use of his first name so publicly in front of these potential suspects. What on earth was his boss up to?

Swann carried on.

"Look around you everyone, note please who is not currently on the stage and, therefore, the only person capable of operating the trap door."

Parker looked astonished again. Then Compton spoke up.

"But Inspector, they're all on stage, at that point in the script all of the characters appear to goad Scrooge into his grave."

"Quite Compton, and isn't that ironic in itself? Although you're quite wrong when you say that everybody's on stage. You're not are you?"

Compton's face flushed red.

"Well, of course not, but you can't be suggesting…"

"Please Mr. Compton I'm suggesting nothing, what possible motive would you have for killing your leading actor? I've watched you boil up an ulcer all night just thinking about the potential financial ruin that faces you. No, I was just proving a point. Not *everybody* is on the stage… are they Mr. Carver?"

Parker gasped and watched the frail figure in the wheelchair twitch in surprise.

"But… of course…" Carver began in a weak, fluttery voice.

"*How dare you! Stand up when an Officer is addressing you, sir!*" Swann screamed at the top of his lungs, making the whole room jump in fear, none more than Carver, who was on his feet in seconds, blankets falling to the floor, wheelchair spinning violently back against the far wall.

"Well now," Swann murmured to himself, "Who would have believed that might actually have worked?"

The room erupted into chaos as everyone, police officers included, began to ask questions at once.

"Please!" Swann shouted, "Please be quiet."

Carver saw his moment and ran towards the stage and the back curtain,

"Lewis!" Swann shouted, but the Constable was already on the move. Carver was quicker however; fear and his old army training serving him well as he placed a violent blow to the policeman's jaw that sent the Welshman tumbling.

The other constables moved in but Carver was backstage before any of them could get close.

Swann grabbed Doctor Milverton.

"Sir, you are arrested as an accomplice! Parker, get after Carver!"

The young sergeant dashed past Swann, and made to give chase.

"The game's afoot, eh sir?"

"You m'boy read too many Penny Dreadfuls, now get after him, I'm right behind you."

After depositing Milverton with a young constable, Swann followed more carefully – partly through an attempt to keep his dignity, and partly because his comparative bulk made it difficult to chase suspects convincingly – making his way carefully across the stage, past the curtain, down the corridor that lead to the dressings rooms, past the green room, and finally to the steps that lead to the back door.

Outside the chill of the night had set in and Swann's breath crystallised in front of his face as he shouted for his partner.

"Parker?" he called, there was no sign of either of them. Concerned he shouted again, "Parker!"

"Down here sir!" came the young man's distant reply.

Swann moved in the direction of the voice, down some steps and along the riverside.

The ghostly spill of the distant gas lamps and the glow of the moon highlighted Parker's silhouette. The River Avon had frozen. Carver staggered on the ice at the midway point, his feet slipping on the damp surface, the young sergeant cautiously making to join him.

"Don't be an idiot Parker!" Swann shouted, puffing at the exertion of running, and grabbing the young man by the shoulder. "You'll end up going under." He pulled Parker back and held onto him to get his breath back for a moment. "That goes for you too Carver! Get back over here and let's talk sensibly shall we?"

"What's the point?" Carver shouted, losing his footing again. "I'll hang and you know it. He's got his own way even from beyond the grave."

He stopped trying to move and just stood there, shoulders sagging in the half-light.

"Just like he always did: the Golden Boy. It never mattered what I did, fighting for King and country, risking my life on a bloody battlefield time and time again. It was always Merrick, Merrick and his marvellous performances! He always had the money, the fame... the women. What did I get? A pitiful pension and a couple of theatrical cast offs."

He turned to face them.

"And do you want to know what really hurt?" he laughed, "He wasn't even any good!"

There was a loud crack and Carver wobbled on his feet.

"Get back here! Quickly man!" Swann shouted.

"Oh... why bother?" Carver hissed, stamping his foot on the creaking ice. He struck a pose in the moonlight.

"*I wear the chain I forged in life. I made it link-by-link and yard-by-yard; and of my own free will I wore it... I cannot rest, I cannot stay, I cannot linger anywhere. In life; my spirit never walked beyond our counting house, never roamed abroad...*"

Carver addressed his audience directly.

"*... now weary journeys lie before me* "

He lowered slowly to a bow and then, in a spray of shattered ice and water, vanished from view into the depths below.

Swann looked doleful in the evening gloom.

"Do you know Parker, he really *was* rather good."

They stared in silence as the spurts of river water through the hole in the ice calmed and, eventually, ceased.

"Awful way to go, sir", said Parker finally.

"Most awful, Parker. Most awful."

At this point Constable Lewis re-appeared, looking a little woozy.

"Ah. Er, I'm sorry about that, sir. I don't really think I've been much use to you on this case…"

Swann clapped his loyal colleague on the shoulder.

"Don't worry, Arthur. Your secret is safe with me."

Lewis went to speak, but Swann interrupted.

"You knew that Roderick was the murderer all the time, and you never said a word, you were just waiting for the right time to pounce."

Lewis tried to speak. "But sir, no. I…"

"Such modesty! You'll probably turn round now and try and deny it! I say, Parker, if only his modesty was as convincing as his courage, what!"

"But I'm not being modest, sir…"

"A remarkable man, sir." Confirmed Parker, playing along, and trying not to grin too hard.

"Remarkable indeed" continued Swann. "He would have laid down his life to catch his man. And I, for one, owe my life to him, for Carver might have killed me at any time." Swann once again puts his arm round the confused Lewis's shoulders.

After a while Lewis pulled away from Swann's embrace. "Well, thank you very much, sir, *sirs*. And now, with your permission, I think I'll close this production down. I've had enough trouble with Ebenezer Scrooge for one year. Last thing we want is Bob Cratchett coming a cropper with that bloody great turkey. Wouldn't you agree, sirs?"

"Humbug," came the joint reply.

Swann & Parker's adventures continue in 'The Crime Of The Crimea' available soon from Humdrumming.

THEATRE

Coming soon to Humdrumming...

BECOMING HOLMES
BY GUY ADAMS - ISBN 1-905532-07-5

Songs from the road...

An actor's life as he tries to stage a revival of 'The Secret Of Sherlock Holmes'; the play originally commissioned by famed Holmes actor Jeremy Brett to celebrate the character's centenary.

This is not a famous actor though; this is not a high profile production company with cash to burn and big contacts to call on. No. This is the cofounder of a company of two, barrelling around the country with their costumes and props in the back of a battered Mondeo. This is the bottom of the theatrical food chain: they've no money and no backup. In fact, most people would say they've no chance at all.

Which just goes to show how little they know...

Part journal, part memoir, Guy Adams' account of theatre against the odds is a humorous, soulful and painfully honest story of obsession, desperation, hair dye and beer. Haunted by the ghosts of an award winning actor, a genius author and his larger than life creation there's no guarantee that he'll make this journey with his sanity or pride intact.

It's a dangerous road to Baker Street and back.

Songs From the Road
Guy Adams

Time broken up in streetlight halos, flashing chevrons and the perpetual whisper of tarmac beneath tyres. It could be the front seat of a Ford Mondeo (with the small scab of a cigarette burn on the upholstery from a sleepy morning and windy day) or the back of a Hire Van, bedding down in the plastic wrapped costumes, the faint afterthought of sweat and smoky working men's clubs clinging to their fabric like oil on a seabird. There's little difference; the memories blend.

In your ears there's the rattle and hum of a nighttime radio station playing songs from other years, nostalgic drive time - all purring guitars and desert-sun vocals - broken up by lethargic competitions where the lost and lonely connect across the medium wave to fight for alarm clocks, tea towels, calculators... junk. Trevor's working the graveyard shift surrounded by empty monitors and a barely thumbed novel, Jane's the night staff at a Nursing Home in the South, Derek's got a freight load of canned fruit that are ferry bound (and god help him if the company catch him using his mobile behind the wheel - but he's got miles to burn and he's damned if he's going to pull over in the name of a BBC Radio T-Shirt).

Part of you engages, solving the anagrams or pop quiz challenges that lie between these contestants and their unwanted prize, but, for the most part, your eyelids hang heavy and the words become meaningless, background noise.

The cash tin rattles on the back seat, your feeble take from another theatrical cross on the map, another line on your tour poster. It might have been good, one more decimal point off the overdraft, but it's just as likely that you'll have little change from a tank of petrol and a couple of night's accommodation (and that'll soon vanish in the theatre bar of your next port of call). You realised this wasn't about the money several hundred miles ago. It can't be, you keep going, keep adding dates and venues, and that way can only lead to poverty (in fact you passed the road sign at your first junction - a tatty wild west tombstone with 'destitution' burned deep and black). This is about the journey.

A crumpled life, a life of disposables, sachets and service stations. Your last meal came vacuum packed, ham and cheese on wholemeal, bought from the gas station two hours ago. The attendant had a puffy cist on his forehead and a wicked sneer on his lips as you asked for a pack of Marlboro ("Twenty Coffin Nails." he hissed slamming the pack on the counter as if peddling kiddie porn) and you were just too damned tired to hate him for it. You kill time at the magazine rack while waiting for the tank to be filled, flicking through glossies, soaking up other lives; daylight faces (why is it that the world seems constant nighttime when you're on tour? Twilight living.)

Then you step out of the neon bubble, through doors that hiss open and closed like dreams, and you're back in the dark, back on the road. Lost in the memory of another performance down, its imperfections and faults, its areas for improvement - mental notes to self. It's true to say that while you physically leave the stage behind your mind never quite follows. You're walking dead and have been for months, only truly alive when you're in front of your audience, those strangers in the dark. At some point on the road - at one of the neon way stations that mark up the miles - you left yourself behind. Now you're more the characters you play than anyone so unimportant and two dimensional as the cipher on your birth certificate. You begin to wonder if you'll find yourself again somewhere down the line, a few miles past the last stage, a hollow ghost hitching on the hard shoulder, thumb out and eyes dark waiting for the ride back to reality; raw meat by the side of the road.

You wonder even more whether you'd recognise that man or just drive on by en route to other stages, other curtains… just another stranger in the dark.

'Becoming Holmes' is due from Humdrumming in 2006.

Cromwell: The Diary Of A Play
Laurence Buxton

AUGUST 14th 2003.

I was working at a wine store in the centre of Stratford-upon-Avon when I first met Steve Newman. He was paying for a bottle of claret (not a bad one either at £7.99), and his quiet, studious air suggested he might, like me, be a writer; although I can't remember now if that was before or after he put a dog-eared manuscript on the counter.

I took the plunge and began to talk to him of my own writing ambitions, and how, despite sending in a stack of ideas to every production company in Britain, I had gotten nowhere. My latest project was a radio play about a school reunion, and immediately Steve suggested I might let him have a look at it. He then gave me his card: "The Bird Of Prey Theatre Company", and off he went with a smile. Well, I thought, nothing ventured, nothing gained. So, after finishing work that night I printed off a copy of the play and sent it off to the address on the card.

It had been a five-minute chat, nothing more, but it had offered me a chance to get to converse with a writer who might just know some of the RSC actors who drank down at the Dirty Duck pub, just a stone's throw from the Royal Shakespeare Theatre. The dead-endedness of my job (and my self belief) had also taught me to grab at each and every opportunity that arose.

On the subject of the job, I had recently discovered that I was being paid, as a trainee manager, less than the man who swept the market place on a Friday night. I would have been even more aghast if I had known that I was about to be given the brush-off by the area manager. Our company, since I had been with them, had gone through more regional managers, area developers, regional training executives, than my customers had bottles of Chinese lager, and to find that my new manager was a ruthless, uncaring swine was almost a relief. Like an old sheepdog lying helplessly awaiting his end I almost looked forward to the sound of the shotgun.

But enough of the real world. Perhaps this Steve Newman might just give me the chance to mix with the likes of the affable actor, John Nettles (of Midsomer Murders fame), and perhaps even put an end to me sending out material that was invariably rejected. Could this man help me turn the corner? Perhaps?

SEPTEMBER 7th 2003.

Having sent off a copy of my radio play to this Newman guy I had, of course, heard nothing. So I dialled the number on the card and left a message in my 'nice' but impatient style, which can be convincingly civil, but only to strangers.

A couple of days later I got a call back from Steve who gave me a calm analysis of the play saying it was good comic stuff. But then came the bit I don't like - criticism. There were too many characters and not enough time in forty-five minutes to develop them all. Two or three would be better. I cut him short there saying I had taken his comments on board. It's not that I can't take criticism, I can, sometimes, but they should be sugar-coated and in moderation. One cannot allow criticism to wield its ugly head too often otherwise the creative juices dry up.

Anyway, Steve gave me an address, The Shrieves House - which sounded faintly familiar - and an invitation to join in rehearsals of his new play. I didn't catch the name of the play, or even the theme, but it sounded very different to mine.

WEDNESDAY 10th SEPTEMBER, 2003.

On entering The Shrieves House I realised I'd walked into a genuine piece of living history. This is one of the finest buildings in Stratford and dates back to the mid-16th Century. Behind the mighty oak door there is a twisting hallway leading to a spacious kitchen that overlooks a courtyard that sees thousands of visitors every year. Each of the main rooms has a separate feel of its own, with the large upstairs living room a mixture of late 19th century elegance and 1930s functional.

Entering the dining room is like being transported back to the 17th century. It is a dark room, with grey flagstone flooring, and a large open fireplace on the far wall that frames a mighty, throne-like chair. The window could be straight out of a haunted house, allowing in just enough light to illuminate a long oak dining table covered with bowls of fruit, cheese, and stone jugs full of wine. As the autumn light fades the subdued lighting helps complete the picture.

Then, having taken all that in, I find myself confronted with the cast. And the first thing I notice is that the chap who owns the house – a big, effervescent character, with long dark hair and a beard – is one of my most loyal customers at the shop: Steve Devey. Steve D is a jolly man who always popped in with his enormous, lovable Newfoundland dog, "Missy" at his side, and always bought a huge selection of liqueurs and wines every week.

There's another chap who looks like a friendly hermit, with a bad tailor, sat on a stool in a darkened corner, with what appears to be an elderly, overweight priest bumbling around him quoting Latin. Somehow it was not what I had been expecting. But I have to ask myself: what exactly *was* I expecting?

Steve Newman makes me at home. I shake his hand, and sit down in the gloom. I hear something from Mr. Devey about the seat I've chosen being the 'haunted' one, and therefore colder than the others. More of his rumour-spreading, I ponder, although having taken my coat off I do end up putting it on again near the end of the evening as it is a bit on the nippy side. Something about this place makes you actually *want* to believe it's true.

I took the copy of the script handed to me by Steve N, *1651: An Evening With Oliver Cromwell*. Hmm. It can't get more historical than that, but everyone seems to have an opinion on the 'warted one', one way or another. Could be interesting.

I find out the names of the other two people in the room – the wild-eyed imp with the beard is called Clive, and the black-robed priest in the huge hat is John Corvin.

"You can be John Bunyan," says Steve Newman.

This is an around the table session, but John is still up on his feet, shuffling about by the window, bellowing his way in a very resonant baritone - which suggests a theatrical heritage - through a holy grace pasted in the big book in front of him. Then the others speak.

Clive imperiously orders the priest to "sit", and allow the guests to eat. What an extraordinary rustic growl he has for such a scrawny guy. Mind I'm not much bigger. Like a whippet with anorexia, me.

Steve – who is Cromwell in every sense – is actually a fine actor, with enormous stage presence, and even though things are at a fairly early stage he's got a very good grasp of the leading role. He could *be* the Lord Protector. He slouches with a combination of arrogance and casual power, and effortlessly shouts down his second-in-command, Major General Harrison. Steve N – as Harrison – combines a certain cheeky one-up-manship over Cromwell, with a crude liking for the ladies. From what I can see – maybe because it's his play – he seems to be more relaxed than Steve D, although his script is open in front of him, unlike Steve D's. Which may explain *why* he's more relaxed.

Anyway, we get to my part, and having heard Steve N – and particularly Steve's slightly difficult-to-place accent – I have a stab at Bunyan. Steve N told me beforehand that Bunyan was born near the River Ouse, and was an infantryman in Cromwell's New Model Army. I have to say I'm curious about the exact truth of this, but Steve N is clearly a historian, and it was he who invited me along, so best not to be too much the clever dick. At least not yet.

And I enjoy it. A holy man is about as far from my own atheist outlook as you could get, but it's not a big part and I get to give a bit of fire and brimstone without overdoing it. Less a volcano, more a small domestic fire. But no sooner have I done this then I find myself reading the part of a Royalist spy. And I find myself gently chided for not being posh enough. I *am* posh. How can I not now do my *own* voice? Like Terry Gilliam not being able to do an American accent for the Python team when requested – despite being their only American!

Well I do it. And the Spy is fiercely questioned by Cromwell and Harrison. This is quite an adrenalin-rush, and having dropped the bombshell that I have had an affair with Elizabeth Cromwell, the daughter of Oliver, and made her pregnant, I'm taken away to be hanged, which is a cover to be a spy for Cromwell, in other words: a double agent.

But before I can be sent back as a spy, I beat up the guard (Bunyan) off-stage and escape, having put Bunyan in my original clothes. Then I narrate a sneering letter that tells how the Spy is, in fact, Prince Charles.

I hope you were paying attention. Because I 'm having trouble getting my head round that myself. Particularly as I'm not sure if I'm playing both Bunyan *and* the Spy – and if I *am*, that means I have to first get apprehended by myself, then club myself unconscious, put myself into my own clothes, and push myself into the front room, before narrating the letter while out cold. Quite a baptism of theatrical fire, I think you would agree.

Still, I try and narrate the letter, which promises vengeance on Cromwell for the death of Charles I – my father. I try and add some extra menace.

"Give it some Christopher Lee", says Steve as he pours himself another glass of red wine. You may have noticed that the grape has as a big part in this play.

But an entertaining evening nonetheless. John Corvin's priest disappeared the moment his short piece was done, which I am told is his modus operandi, yet to be fair to him, he leaves an indelible memory. And as for Clive? Well, he is quite a one-off, and a bit like a wandering soothsayer from a bygone age, with his characterisation of the Family Retainer clearly borne of many years playing such roles, and playing them brilliantly. While John seems to have his own way of behaving – and departing – separate to the group, Clive seems to be a team player, and loyal to Steve N. But he's a bit of a mystery.

So I take my leave, in a little bit of a daze, hopefully having increased my contacts, I'm now going to be getting into someone else's skin. But I was never good at learning things short-term, so how am I going to get my head round the part of Bunyan – or, possibly, that of the future King?

Laurence Buxton's journal will be available from Humdrumming in the new year.

Putting On Plays
Steve Newman

Think of Stratford-upon-Avon and you think William Shakespeare, or the Royal Shakespeare Theatre, which is one in the same thing really, and something that doesn't leave much room for any other theatre. Which suggests I was completely off my head back in 1997 when I created - with two other Stratford playwrights - The Bird of Prey Theatre Company, a small professional theatre company dedicated to new writing. The BBC thought I was mad too.

" But you don't start small professional theatre companies these days. Just not done, old chap."

I ignored them, of course, and the three of us, bolstered by a few (a good few) pints of Flowers Best Bitter began a course of action that was to take over my life for the next few years.

My first play for BoP was about the American poet, Walt Whitman, who is a hero of mine, and not just for his poetry but for his outspokenness on the horrors and hypocrisy of slavery, his open attitude to sex, and the importance of social inclusion - at a time when such opinions were at the very least unwelcome - also for his unashamed and genuine patriotism, and his huge bravery and selflessness during the American Civil War..

When I discovered his work in the early 1960s I had no idea who he was, but knew I wanted to write about him. But how, and in what way? By the mid 1990s, with one play produced, and another commissioned, I knew the only way I could bring the man to life was by putting him on a stage. But how do you write a play about an American poetic icon?

I started by reading even more plays than I usually did to rediscover there is no set way to write anything, especially drama. After ploughing my way through Pinter, and Arthur Miller - who were of little help - and Terrence Rattigan, who gave me some hope - especially with his play, Ross, about T.E. Lawrence - I came across the playwright who, in the end, gave me the most inspiration: the English dramatist, John Drinkwater.

A couple of years earlier I'd invested £16 in a two volume, 1st Edition set of Drinkwater's Collected Plays (published 1925), and found the inspiration I needed in his two American Civil War pieces, Abraham Lincoln (1918) and Robert E. Lee (1923). I believe these two plays show Drinkwater at his best. He immediately gets to grips with his title character, and how they became who they became.

This was what I wanted to try and do with my Whitman piece, get a real feel of the poet, of his emotions, and beliefs, in short telling speeches and exchanges that quickly make an audience believe they are in the presence of the man himself, at the same time making him (hopefully) relevant to a modern audience who are faced with some of the same problems. And, as a writer with a certain sense of responsibility, I had to decide early whether or not to use the word 'nigger'. That I chose to do so, in its historical context, brought me a good deal of grief and criticism from many who thought I was simply perpetuating the hatred that Whitman himself had fought 150 years earlier. Tosh of course, but I was called a racist by more than one in the audience who, I feel, should have known better. Such is the lot of the playwright I suppose, as I'm sure Drinkwater knew only too well.

So, with Drinkwater's posthumous encouragement, I slowly started to write my play, Ancient Pinnacles, with the sounds, and the sights, the emotions, the music, and the words of my two characters building into what I hoped would be a thoughtful, yet funny, piece about Walt Whitman on the last day of his life in March 1892, who is visited by a younger version of himself, who in turn became anyone I chose, and take the old poet on a journey of remembrance and discovery that is both funny, and, in places, very painful.

I tried desperately to get inside the head of Whitman - and my own head - to see how he, and I, might react to certain circumstances, and by so doing engage the audience in a similar journey into their own heads where they might tackle their own emotions, loves, and hates. I wanted to create a 'real' Walt Whitman: a man the audience could not only see, and hear, but smell, and touch.

The play was finished in early 1998, and it didn't take me long to cast it either.

I had been watching the work of two local professional actors who I knew were ideal for the play. When I spoke to them they were both keen to have a go, but rightly concerned about the amount of time it would take to learn, and rehearse. In the end I convinced them and the process began.

Peter Cubitt, although a professional actor, works as a teacher, and only devotes his long vacations to acting. I asked him at just the right time and he was therefore able to give what acting time he had in 1998 to Ancient Pinnacles. I also knew that his striking resemblance to Whitman (minus the beard), and comedic talents, would create something very special.

Tim Guest is a young professional actor who, to eat, worked front of house at the RST, but was keen to be part of something new. And having seen him in an amateur production that only used half of his full potential I knew he was ideal as the cocky type of character I needed to goad the dying poet into life again.

We rehearsed in the local Methodist Hall, with Peter and Tim creating a rapport that was truly remarkable, and something I shall remember for the rest of my life. All I had to do as the director was watch them tear verbal chunks out of each other as they faced many of the unpalatable truths about the man that was Walt Whitman. Or laugh until I cried as they became Sir Henry Irving, and Ellen Terry acting Shakespeare very, very, badly, or Henry Longfellow and Whitman telling bawdy tales, and drinking brandy, with Longfellow (who would have preferred to be Whitman) recounting a tale about how he came across two lovers in the hills above Pompeii in the 1860s, and pretending to the couple, when discovered, that he is in fact Whitman. Longfellow - the acclaimed academic and darling of the Boston literary circle - would probably have given all of that up to have written one poem as good as one by Whitman. They became firm friends, but met only twice.

As the rehearsals progressed I would also find my own emotions - and tears - rising as Peter and Tim began to explore in some depth the compassion that was at the heart of Whitman, or found something in my text - or Whitman's poetry - that I had not realised was there. It was both an exhilarating, and exhausting, experience for all of us, but one that, on the first night, exploded in an acting tour de force! It took about two hours, and several pints of Flower's best, for the adrenalin to subside.

Whitman's charming biographer, Philip Callow - who is also a distinguished novelist and poet - came to the first night, and over a glass of wine in the interval complained that I had only portrayed the more upbeat, masculine side of the poet's character. By the end of the show he congratulated me warmly on a job well done, which I felt was high praise indeed from a man who knows Whitman inside out.

The local press rather liked it too, although the Stratford Herald praised the acting but condemned me for apparently trying to suggest - by having the audacity to write about Whitman in the first place I suppose - that I considered myself the American's equal, and that the play didn't tell her - the critic – any more about the man than she knew before, which she also admitted was very little indeed. I won't try and work that one out.

The weekly British newspaper of the entertainment industry, The Stage, thought it was a "...good two-hander." I was happy with that.

Getting Ancient Pinnacles up and running was something of a breakthrough, and I have to admit that the positive critical reception the play received made me even keener to come up with a play that might equal Ancient Pinnacles. What I actually came up with was a kind of sequel.

When the critic of the Stratford Standard wrote that, "...with almost magical inspiration Steve Newman brings out all the joys and tragedies of a nation struggling to find itself..." I was firstly very flattered, and when I challenged him one night to admit he'd been just a little too fulsome in his praise he was, quite rightly, very indignant. I apologised (he's a big man) and bought him a pint. Over the ensuing months we became friends - I even discovered a liking for the piano-accordion, an instrument he played well - and he taught me to never question what a critic says - even if it is the biggest load of rubbish going - because it's bad form.

What he'd actually done was remind me that Whitman's story is the story of America in the 19th century, of the joys and tragedies, the blossoming of literature, art, music, and theatre; but also the aforementioned horrors and hypocrisy of slavery, and the viciousness, and the historical necessity - as both Lincoln and Whitman correctly understood it - of the American Civil War.

I now realised that the sequel to Ancient Pinnacles had to be a play that had its roots in that golden period after Whitman's death in 1892, but which then explores the development of art in the 20th century, and the crushing counterweight of flawed personalities, and the insidious, deathly creep of political dictatorship, world war, and mass murder. I had my plan, but how to showcase it? I decided to create two fictional characters.

Well, to be honest, I initially wanted to write a play about the abstract expressionist, Jackson Pollock, and use him in the way I had Whitman. But after reading Steven Naifeh and Gregory White Smith's superb biography of the artist there was almost too much material, and the fragmented, often lunatic, character of Pollock too self-centred to use as a conduit of the 20th century. The Pollock Estate was also very protective of its man, and at the time I didn't want to go down the bumpy road of seeking permission for every bloody word and thought.

After a great deal of contemplation, and false starts, I decided to present two fictional characters as real people - one a painter, the other a sculptor - even to the extent of giving them biographies, which, when coupled with the action on stage - and the real people they came into contact with - created a wonderful sense of verisimilitude, making a good proportion of the audience believe in the characters of Max Jackson and Rosemary Leonard.

The title, Portrait of the Artist, fitted the bill easily as it is perhaps one of the most used in the 20th century, with perhaps the most familiar being James Joyce's Portrait of the Artist as a Young Man, and Dylan Thomas's Portrait of the Artist as a Young Dog, the best known. It was a good literary model to follow.

I did hang on to Pollock's extremely fragile mental state - and his genius - but added a further, unenviable mix of the sardonic, sarcastic Orson Welles; Scott Fitzgerald on a volatile bender; with just a smidgen of that most accomplished, yet flawed of jazz musicians, Bix Beiderbecke. To complete my Mad Max I added just a smattering of John Wayne at his most immobile; a slice of Hemingway's ego; a thimble full of Paul Robeson's huge kindness; and to top him off, just a shake or two of the Mexican artist, Diego Rivera, to add a little spice. There could be no doubt that Max Jackson would go down - as he must - screaming and kicking.

The creation of Rosemary Leonard, as a necessary female balance to Max, had to be an assured artist with a convoluted background that would give me every opportunity to zip backwards and forwards in time. I'd been reading Margaret Gardiner's lovely book about the English sculptor, Barbara Hepworth, and had recently visited Hepworth's studio and gardens in St Ives, Cornwall, and knew her self-assured existence, and artistic ruthlessness would be an ideal model for Rosemary. No way was this play going to be PC.

As with Max I needed to add certain emotional, and physical elements, to give Rosemary a much more multi-faceted appeal, so in went a generous helping of the legendary American painter, Georgia O'Keefe; the outspoken, no nonsense, yet ultimately tragic jazz diva, Bessie Smith; with a little sprinkling of the Mexican artist, Frida Karlo (who was Diego Rivera's wife of course, and a nice touch on my part I thought); plus the professionalism of the journalist, Martha Gellhorn; all held together by the inscrutability of Eleanor Roosevelt. There could be no doubt Rosemary would spend her entire, and very long life, screaming and kicking.

Portrait of the Artist is not a straight forward narrative - life is not a straight forward narrative - but a look at the last 120 years through the eyes of many different people, at different times, and in different places. One minute it is 1907, and we are in the Lancashire seaside town of Southport; then we find ourselves in 1930s Paris, and New York, before (via a New England mental hospital) we land in Spain during the civil war. Then, after witnessing, in 1911, the murder of one half of a vaudeville act we shout and scream for blood during a famous 1920s boxing match at Madison Square Garden, before Nazi Germany, and Hitler, elbow their way into the narrative.

And although the play has many characters, with some portrayed at different stages of their lives, the play can only, must only, have two actors.

All drama runs on high octane energy, and a play with only two actors has to consume huge amounts of this energy, with the nearest usable source being the other actor, and if you are really lucky, the audience as well. On a good night the results can be electrifying, as they were to be with Portrait of the Artist.
The play was produced in June 1999, with Allen Maslen as Max, and Sue Davison as Rosemary.

The first couple of rehearsals were rather stiff and unproductive affairs, with Sue and Allen almost avoiding each other. Something had to be done. I decided to concentrate on a scene that not only require split second acting skills, but also singing and dancing skills too.

Bob & Belle are an invented turn of the century vaudeville act - based very loosely on Bert Lahr & Mercedes - but unlike that famous duo, Bob & Belle are bad, very bad. I hoped that by trying to get Sue and Allen to become a very bad vaudeville act they might start to communicate, and get the energy flowing. And it worked, with each trying to show the other how to sing and dance badly, and deliver my dreadful jokes.
BOB: Belle? My dogs got no nose.
BELLE: Your dogs got no nose? How does he smell?
BOB: Awful!
And so on.
The secret was to make it almost funny, but at the same time very sad, in the sense that we watching an act, and two people, on the skids. There had to be an edge of despair, yet an overriding sense of professionalism (no matter how bad the act) in the execution of the routine. We spent several days of rehearsals on that scene until Sue and Allen became Bob & Belle. We then worked outwards from the scene to the start, and the end of the play.

As with Ancient Pinnacles it was a joy to see the play coming together, and be amazed at the dexterity and passion of the two people on stage, and how they were able, in a split second, to become someone else, or an older, or younger, version of a character. I shall be eternally grateful to Sue and Allen for making those two dreadfully wonderful creations of mine come alive.
Again, the play was produced at The Shakespeare Institute, but this time in the round - whereas Ancient Pinnacles had been staged at one end - which made the whole thing even more intimate, especially when, in a half light, Sue and Allen simulated an extremely convincing sexual act, or committed murder, or roared around the space in almost uncontrollable moments of madness, or became boxers, or, in the case of Allen, Hitler. All good stuff.

As with the Whitman piece, Portrait of the Artist did seem to make people think about their lives, and those that influence them, it also made then laugh (which is always good), and, as I've said before, make some people believe that Max and Rosemary really had existed, which was a bit of bind in the pub afterwards when an elderly member of the audience came up to me and insisted he actually knew Max Jackson. I'd have gone along with it too had he bought me a drink.

My next project was the direction of a mad comedy (by an American playwright) called Shrink Resistant. After a couple of weeks of rehearsals two of the young actors decided to pull out and get jobs as waiters, plus another told me he'd been given the chance of a part in a leading TV soap of the day and, "...just had to say yes, darling." So off he went to soap oblivion, and a £500,000 penthouse apartment somewhere in London's Dockland. I was, of course, completely, and utterly, buggered. That is until I remembered a young man by the name of Guy Adams. I called him and we arranged to meet for a drink at the Dirty Duck.

Guy is a cross between an Edwardian gentleman who may once have known Oscar Wilde, and Oscar Wilde himself. He is also a world authority on Dr Who, and was, when I first met him, a 25 year old actor and novelist with a reputation for playing heavies on day time television. I soon came to realise that he is one of the funniest and most convivial men alive, an actor of remarkable talent and range, and a delight to work with. He is also completely dependable, imaginative, outspoken, outrageous, and as camp as coffee. He delighted in wearing frock coats, and gaudy waistcoats, and addressing pub landlords as: "My good man.", which is a bit of a risk in a few Stratford pubs, believe me. And when not explaining, in depth, the finer points of Tom Baker's approach to playing Dr Who he smokes too much, and has one of the deepest pockets I know when it comes to buying drinks. In other words he is an all round good egg. I explained my predicament to him and he immediately agreed to play two parts in the daft comedy. So far, so good. But I needed someone else.

It was then, on the Monday morning, that I received a very polite letter from a 22 year old Phil Jarrett who, after apologising for taking-up my valuable time (I loved him already) wanted to know if I had any work for a young actor, and musician, of outstanding talent, namely himself? Did I have any work, did I have any work? As Bilko might have said. Within a week Phil had left his shared flat in London and moved up to Stratford and in with Guy. It was the start of a great friendship, and working partnership, for all three of us.

As soon as Shrink Resistant finished in that August of 2000 we went straight into rehearsals for my play, A Summer Garden, where Phil Jarrett played Sir Edward Elgar, with Guy creating a wonderful George Bernard Shaw (I took Shaw out of the later version of the play), with West End stalwart, Chris Briggs, playing the wheelchair bound Frederick Delius to such effect that several members of the Delius Society, who came to see the show, thought they'd seen a ghost.

The action of A Summer Garden takes place in the garden of the English composer, Frederick Delius, at his home at Grez-Sur-Loing, south of Paris, on the afternoon of Tuesday May 30th 1933. Delius is paralysed and partially blind as a result of syphilis. Sir Edward Elgar has flown to France (his first flight) to conduct a performance of his Violin Concerto with the young Yehudi Menuhin. After lunch with the Menuhin family Elgar decides to drive down to Grez and call on his musical friend and contemporary. The meeting between Elgar, Delius, and Jelka Delius (Delius's long suffering artist wife) is, in A Summer Garden, an emotional, 'explosive', and often funny journey into their secret and public lives, and into the political and social tensions of the early 1930s, and how England's two most eminent composers - from very different backgrounds - longed for times irrevocably gone. And when the play was produced in 2000 - and again in 2003 - the response was, thankfully, quite overwhelming.

But what to do in 2001?

Then, early in 2001, I heard about the RSC's plans to build a temporary theatre in the car park of the RST, between the theatre, and the Bancroft Gardens. I decided we had to get a couple of shows into that space, but how, and which ones? There wasn't time to get my new play about Ernest Hemingway finished and ready. I spoke about it with Guy and Phil and we agreed to put on Ancient Pinnacles and Portrait of the Artist again.

Of course the RSC was no stranger to me, in fact my 'association' with the RSC goes back to the pre-RSC days of 1959 when, as an eleven year old, I would sit in the cafeteria overlooking the river and drink a banana milkshake and then look at the photographs of Laurence Olivier and Paul Robeson in the foyer, and feel better about things. In the 1960s I would often sit outside the theatre watching the comings and goings of such actors as Peter O'Toole, or watch Peter Hall arrive in his green Jaguar XK120 sports car, with the gorgeous Leslie Caron at his side. The RST was a kind of bastion for me against what appeared to be an uncaring, out-dated nation, with Stratford itself a prime example of such petrified attitudes. But with Hall now running the theatre I felt there was a chance that things just might change. The RSC was the local equivalent of having Peter Cook and Dudley Moore on your doorstep, and on your side.

By the 1990s I was extremely lucky to appear in Sir Peter Hall's RSC production of Julius Caesar where, during rehearsals late one night I was also bold enough to suggest to the great man I might incorporate a 'bit of business' with Caesar's bloody cloak. My suggestion was that as Hugh Quarshie (as Mark Anthony), now wearing Caesar's blood stained cloak, addresses the crowd thus:
" O, mighty Caesar! Dost thou lie so low?
  Are all they conquests, glories, triumphs, spoils,
  Shrunk to this little measure..."
I should reach out and touch the blood stained garment. "What do you think, Sir Peter?"
"Try it." shouted Hall from the gloom of the stalls. And as I did so Hugh stopped his address and watched me touch Caesar's blood with my fingers, and then, in a much lower, and tremulous voice, continued:
"I know not, gentlemen, what you intend,
  Who else must be let blood..."
And so on. Hall liked it, and it stayed in for the 70 performances, and on tour afterwards, with someone else touching the bloody cloak.

So, not being the sort of chap to let old connections cool, myself and Guy started telephoning the RSC to find out how we could get our two shows into their temporary new theatre, now christened The RSC Summerhouse. I have to say the response was less than deafening, but we kept on trying, and eventually made contact with a young woman who was one of the coordinators. She took details and promised to get back to us. In the meantime we began rehearsals in a small barn on the edge of the Cotswolds.

The barn was owned by Mark and Belinda Roberts, a wonderfully eccentric couple who'd transformed an old barn into a private theatre where Belinda staged her own, very funny, plays for children. It was an ideal place to rehearse, and after a couple weeks I suggested to Belinda and Mark that it might be possible to stage both plays in the barn to a non-paying invited audience who could then have a drink with us afterwards and, by so doing, spread the word, and our hopes, for the RSC

Summerhouse. Mark and Belinda readily agreed, and both shows (played over a couple of weeks) were well received, with drinks in the garden afterwards a good way to get to know people, and enjoy some beautiful summer evenings.

While we waited we booked both shows into Cox's Yard (an old timber yard that had closed some years earlier) that was now a pub and restaurant complex, with a small conference-cum-performance space, where we played both shows alternately over a couple of weeks to good audiences and good reviews.

Mind you the RSC were not too happy that we had effectively 'opened' at Cox's Yard. But they soon swallowed their pride and booked us into The Summerhouse for September 26th and October 3rd 2001.

On September the 11th the World Trade Centre Towers were attacked and the heart went out of our enterprise for a while. In fact I thought of cancelling the shows until I was persuaded out of it by the interest there seemed to be in the plays, especially the Whitman piece. And a lot of American tourists did come to see that show, and hopefully found some solace in a play that was very much about the American dream, and to no little extent the nightmare too.

Both productions were very different to the originals, with Guy and Phil playing Whitman, and his mysterious visitor, in a much more up-beat, and humorous fashion that did, no question about it, highlight the more emotionally telling moments. With Phil a very accomplished guitar player I made Whitman a guitar player too, and introduced a couple of songs that went down very well.

Again, with Portrait of the Artist Max Jackson, played by Guy, and Rosemary Leonard, played by Sophia Bradley, came out very differently to the original production. For instance, in the original, thirty something Sue Davison played her seven year old self more as a memory of childhood than anything else, whereas seventeen year old Sophia actually became the seven year old Rosemary. It was an amazing transformation, and just goes to show there is seldom, if ever, a definitive performance of anything. Although Phil didn't actually appear in Portrait he was certainly heard. Whereas we'd used recorded music for the first production, for this we used music specially written by Phil (plus one recorded piece) which he performed on both acoustic, and electric guitars, at the same time playing the drums where required. I'm not sure which was more entertaining: the play, or watching Phil trying to remember his music cues?

It has to be said that The Summerhouse was not an ideal venue, nor did things always go to plan, as Guy Adams explains:

"Working the RSC Summerhouse should (and perhaps could?) have been a real career high for BoP and, indeed, myself. Sadly my main memories of the two shows there concern the constant battle against beer glasses and geese. The 'tent' was split in half with a thin sheet partition designed to keep the tiered performance area apart from the bar. This it succeeded in geographically, if not aurally. The performance was backed throughout with the persistent clatter and crash that always goes hand in hand with a bar - especially one, in their wisdom, the RSC had decided to keep open. My attempts to inveigle myself soulfully into the withered heart of our fictional Whitman (and by extension the audience) was often hampered therefore by some git shouting, 'Two pints of Stella and a packet of dry roasted please darling.'

"When it came to our second show, Portrait of the Artist it was the screeching of the Canada Geese bobbing up and down on the Avon just outside that threatened to drown out co-actor (and girlfriend at the time), Sophia Bradley and myself in our whistle-stop tour of art and life in the twentieth century.

" I was, by necessity, having to commit two full scripts to memory so when it came to a section in Portrait where I recited a Hitler speech to the glorious sound of Benny Goodman's Carnegie Hall recording of, 'Sing, Sing, Sing' I chose the lazy route of pinning the two sheets of script to my lectern and reading it.

"During the first half of the show I'd started to experience extreme discomfort in my right eye. I'm very short sighted and one of the contact lenses I was wearing had split. Removing it during the interval solved the pain but had the result that I couldn't see properly for the rest of the performance. I had completely forgotten about the speech of course.

"As I walked toward the lectern I was racking my brains for the lines. I couldn't even come up with the first sentence. The music played, I leaned on the lectern, eyeballed the audience and wondered what to do. Dropping my head down to my chest, and holding a demonstrative arm out to cover my trickery, I closed one eye - clarifying my lopsided vision - and quickly scanned the opening paragraph. I was away! The trick was repeated. I had the smug satisfaction of discovering later that nobody noticed.

" Both shows will always be very personal to me, not only as great pieces of theatre but as great challenges, and works that had to fight their way into the attention of a theatre audience gluttoned by the RSC. I like to think we managed. We took people on a journey, which is what all storytelling should be about."

As Guy said, it was a journey, and a terrific one at that, and one I shall never forget, or regret. And how many playwrights get likened to both Dennis Potter and Quentin Tarantino in one review?

At a dinner party at Steve Devey's in 2003 Steve and I began to talk about our shared interest in the English Civil War. He suggested that I should write a play about Cromwell, and that it should, somehow, be staged at The Shrieves House (where we were having dinner) in Stratford-upon-Avon, because it was thought that Cromwell may have stayed there.

It was a challenge, and during a two week stay in North Wales, in the summer of 2003, I wrote what was initially 1651: An Evening With Oliver Cromwell, which has now become Cromwell: The Play.

But it was that dinner party that gave me the idea of setting the play around a dining table, with the audience guests sharing a meal with Oliver Cromwell and Major General Thomas Harrison, all served by the old family retainer, Jeremiah Beckett, plus several surprise guests.

The play is set a few days before the battle of Worcester in 1651, when Cromwell, and his army of 30,000 men, stayed in and around Stratford on their way to Worcester to destroy Prince Charles and his mercenary army. And the play, using a mixture of fictional melodrama, historical fact, and several thrilling and murderous episodes, does try to get at the heart of Cromwell the politician, soldier, and father. There are also spies, songs, and many surprises.

1651: An Evening With Oliver Cromwell played many times at The Shrieves House, and again in a couple of Stratford hotels, and in a local Catholic retreat for a large group of schoolchildren, and all to great acclaim.

It is an adaptable piece of work that obviously works well around a large table, or alternatively, can be staged with the table as a centre piece, where Cromwell and Harrison, and the rest of them, can slog it out to their heart's content, watched by an audience in a conventional way.

So, was it worth doing what the BBC said I shouldn't, perhaps even couldn't do? You bet it was, and if I'd listened to them, and thought the RSC to be all powerful, and unapproachable, my plays might never have been written.

All of the plays discussed in Steve Newman's article will be available in the new year from Humdrumming..

Portrait of the Artist - ISBN 1-905532-08-3
When Max Jackson and Rosemary Leonard met in Paris in the 1930s nothing was ever going to be the same again.

American painter, Max is a man who hangs onto life, and sanity, by his finger nails. He is a danger to himself and to anyone who comes into contact with him, especially if he falls in love.

English sculptor, Rosemary, has a past that haunts her every move, her every thought. Nothing is more important to Rosemary than Rosemary, even when she falls in love.

Portrait of the Artist is a love story, and guided tour of the 20th century, of its joys, its music, its sexuality, its politics, and its art. Get on the bus if you dare.

A Summer Garden - ISBN 1-905532-09-1
It is the afternoon of Tuesday May 30th 1933 and Sir Edward Elgar and Frederick Delius meet in the garden of Delius's home in the French village of Grez-sur-Loing.

Delius is paralysed and partially blind as a result of syphilis, with the upright and confident Sir Edward - who is in pain from cancer - ready, as ever, to drink champagne and have some fun.

The meeting between these two men, and Delius's wife, Jelka, is an emotional, funny, and at times heart wrenching journey into their secret lives.

A Summer Garden is also a play that looks at the social and human consequences of war, and the political and social tensions of the mid 1930s.

Ancient Pinnacles - ISBN 1-905532-10-5

It is March 26th 1892, the day of Walt Whitman's death. It will be the longest day of his life.

As dawn breaks the old grey poet is 'visited' by a young stranger who forces the old man to relive his past in a roller-coaster of a ride that takes him back to his childhood, to the New Orleans of 1848 and the slave auctions, to the Brooklyn of the 1850s, and Pfaff's Bar off Broadway, and the Phrenology Cabinet of Fowler & Wells, and the tragedy of the American Civil War.

All aboard! All aboard!

Cromwell: The Play - ISBN 1-905532-11-3

It is the night of August the 27th 1651, just a few days before the battle of Worcester where Oliver Cromwell finally sends the King Pretender, Prince Charles, running for his life, and a night when he and Major General Thomas Harrison join some unsuspecting guests for supper.

But this is no ordinary meal, this is something more akin to a last supper where bread, hearts, and heads are broken, and the past comes to haunt Harrison and Cromwell.

It is also a story of intrigue and espionage, of song and sexual encounters, of betrayal and torture, all of which must finally be reckoned with.

Above all else it is a story of love, of hope, and of faith during the English Civil War; and a play that shows Oliver Cromwell as a man.

Across The River - ISBN 1-905532-12-1

This play is not strictly a dramatic biography of Ernest Hemingway, but a look at the man in relation to his times, and the influences of his grandfather, his mother, and such friends as Scott and Zelda Fitzgerald, James and Nora Joyce, and the iconoclastic Gertrude Stein.

The play also looks at the stormy relationships he had with three of his wives, and the surreal US Army interrogation (virtually a courts martial) that Hemingway was subjected to in October 1944, an event which changed forever the foolish, lovable, bombastic, generous, fearful, brave, cruel, kind, gregarious, and lonely man that was Ernest Hemingway.

SERIALS

The Serials:

An old format brought bang up to date.

These are not novels sliced up piecemeal and drip fed over the weeks; these are honest to god serial adventures – episodic epics - that are available via online subscription. Every week you will receive an e-mail alerting you that the next instalment is available for download from your account page, illustrated 'pdf' files that you can read onscreen or print off and enjoy in whichever easy chair, hammock or toilet seat takes your fancy.

Currently there are two serials on offer, Guy Adams' *The Organization* – a slap bang metaphysical adventure with enough explosions, fight scenes and bizarre humour to keep most mental patients happy – and Steve Newman's *Going the Other Way from Home* – a thrilling drama documentary about the life of Ernest Hemingway.

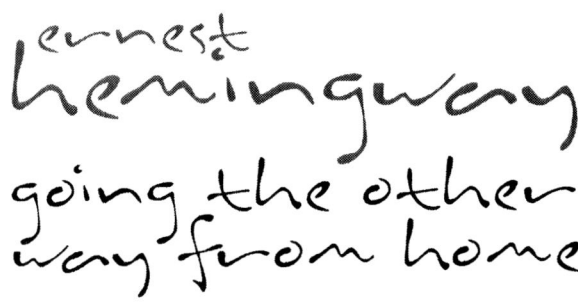

ernest hemingway going the other way from home

by Steve Newman

Hanging onto the wheelhouse rail of the LCVP (Landing Craft, Vehicle and Personnel) as it pitched and rolled in the heavy seas of the English Channel, a dreadfully nauseous, hungover, and exhausted Ernest Hemingway had every intention of landing on Omaha Beach.

Two months earlier Hemingway had been sailing his beloved boat *Pilar* in the no less rough, but warmer waters of the Gulf of Mexico looking for German submarines.

Martha Gellhorn, the distinguished American journalist - and Mrs Ernest Hemingway the third - had scoffed at her husband's original idea to go fishing for U-Boats, instructing him very loudly in her clipped and educated St Louis way - and in front of all the other drinkers at Havana's smart Floridita Bar - that it was all a complete waste of his time, talent, and energy, and that he should be reporting the European war - as she was about to do - unless of course he'd lost his nerve. Hemingway told her she was a lush and to shut her big beautiful mouth otherwise he'd shut it for her. Martha emptied the remains of her Martini over Ernest's head and marched out. She then drove his brand new Lincoln Continental very deliberately, and very carefully, into a tree. A day later she took a flight to New York, and a couple of weeks after that a Norwegian freighter to Liverpool.

Ernest Hemingway did go fishing for U-Boats, and with $500 a month in his pocket, courtesy of the Cuban branch of the FBI - most of which was spent on booze - it proved to be just as much fun as hooking the big Marlins. Needless to say Hemingway and his five man crew never did find any subs - although there were quite a few operating in the area - but had a great time fishing with hand grenades and taking the tops out of palm trees with a heavy machine gun.

In the end Hemingway realized he was wasting his time looking for the elusive U-Boats - they probably heard him coming - and got himself on the next scheduled flying boat from New York, via Shannon, to Southampton, England.

His fame also ensured he took top billing with his old employer *Collier's Weekly*, and very quickly became "embedded" with the US Forces massing along the south coast of England ready for the invasion of France.

Martha Gellhorn wasn't so fortunate. Having spent twenty days on the Norwegian freighter - which was part of a large convoy - watching ships torpedoed and sunk all around her, Martha discovered when she finally reached London that female correspondents were not allowed anywhere near the invasion forces. As someone who had witnessed first hand the brutal Spanish Civil War, and the war in China, Martha gave the rather embarrassed press liaison officer a stern lecture and then headed south to the coast.

After charming her way past an MP she stole aboard a hospital ship and locked herself in a toilet. When, at dawn, the ship began to move, Martha dressed herself in a medics uniform she found in an empty cabin and started helping with the preparations. When the first casualties - American and German - came aboard, the knowledge she had gleaned from her doctor father came in very useful, and as a fluent German speaker she was able to comfort, and ease the distress of the German wounded, and when necessary command them to be quiet.

Now, as Hemingway watched the vomit and sea water slosh around the boots of the GIs crammed into the front of the LCVP he wished he was back in those warm dark seas, or on his farm, the Finca Viga, just outside Havana, with his cats and dogs, and the Martha he'd loved more than anyone except Hadley.

Forty-four year old Oak Park born Ernest Miller Hemingway, famous writer, infamous drinker, big game hunter, would be bullfighter, womanizer, deep sea fisherman, and now an accredited war correspondent with the magazine *Collier's Weekly* likened the New Orleans built LCVPs (Higgins Boats) to "damned iron bathtubs" as his own LCVP - commanded by a young US Navy Lieutenant, Robert Anderson - headed relentlessly toward the increasingly smoke shrouded Omaha Beach. As they did so, a deadly assortment of high explosive shells - fired from the guns of the old battleships *Texas, Arkansas,* and *Nevada* - screamed continually overhead.

As Hemingway observed the beach activity through his binoculars the pain in his head was excruciating. It was his own fault, he realized that, but to have gone back into the hospital to have the fifty seven stitches removed, as the doctor advised, would have meant the possibility of missing the invasion. And as he watched the almost continuous explosions of the shells from the old First World War battleships hitting the German positions, Hemingway vowed never again to take a car ride in a blacked-out London especially with someone whose driving skills had proven to be far inferior to their drinking skills. When the 1937 Humber ploughed into a huge steel water tank Hemingway went crashing head first through the windscreen.

When Martha went to visit her husband in hospital her laughter, at seeing Ernest's head bound in swaths of bandages like a huge turban, didn't help restore his good humour, neither did her criticism of his drinking habits, and dubious drinking companions. Hemingway accused her of not caring about him anymore. Martha didn't disagree, just lit a cigarette, ate Hemingway's grapes, and told him to get his beard trimmed. The marriage was over.

To try and ease the pain in his badly damaged head Hemingway took another slug of brandy from a hip flask, then vomited violently over the side of the LCVP. Okay Doc, he thought, you're right, don't mix booze with pain-killers. Only when he'd finished retching did he notice the wax-grey faces of some of the GIs looking up at him, who he thought rather resembled, under their glistening steel helmets, pikemen from the Middle Ages. He threw the hip flask down to them.

"Thanks Mac."

" It's Napoleon."

" Guy up there says he's Napoleon."

" Goddam world's full of stinkin' generals."

The average age of those wax-grey pikemen was just 24, and they knew well enough what was in store for them as the LCVP churned its diesel stinking way toward the shore and the hell that was being unleashed on their comrades. Most of them just looked down at their feet, some prayed, others read letters from wives or girlfriends for the hundredth time, all of them carried packs weighing over 100 pounds on their backs, all of them were afraid.

Fear gripped Hemingway too as he looked toward the shore. Fear, and the memory of his own baptism of fire in Italy during the last year of the First World War.

He was only 19, and had been away from Oak Park for less than a year driving a Red Cross ambulance, firstly in France, then in Italy. It was the greatest experience of his life, and the Italian soldiers adopted him as something of a mascot. Hemingway couldn't do enough for those kind, generous, and honest men.

Although he didn't have to, Ernest took on the job of delivering mail, wine, cigarettes, and chocolate to the front line on the south western side of the Piave River, in the valley of the Dolomites, and in range of the Austrian artillery.

On one such occasion Ernest had cycled to the front line to begin distributing his goodies when an Austrian Minenwerfer mortar came in high across the river Piave and into the area just in front of a trench Hemingway was heading for. The mortar, exploding with a devastating red hot force like a furnace door opening, scattered its bone splintering deadly cargo of scrap metal. The force of the explosion was like a hurricane, and Hemingway, along with a dozen or more Italian soldiers, took the full blast. Hemingway had been badly injured in the leg and for a long time was unable to move. Gradually he was able to free himself from beneath the dead, and hearing a man crying close at hand, crawled agonizingly toward the sound. When he found the injured man, the young Hemingway, with almost super human strength, got to his feet, hoisted the injured soldier over his shoulder and made for the relative safety of the Italian trenches, where he collapsed.

When the wounded and glamorous young American ambulance driver awoke in a Milan military hospital bed he was greeted by a beautiful young American nurse called Agnes Hannah von Kurowsky. They soon fell deeply in love and every night Agnes was on duty she brought wine to his room and they made love. And afterwards he'd tell her how, when the war was over, they'd marry and live in Spain or France and how he would become a great and famous writer.

"Yes Ernest."

" But I will…"

" Make love to me again Ernest, before the Major makes his rounds."

" The Major knows, he'll leave us alone, he comes from a good family."

Hemingway's reveries were soon interrupted as two German shells exploded alongside the hull of the LCVP, with the huge plumes of water soaking everyone on board. Hemingway shouted and pointed, "Andy you're too far to the right, the church is over there, look. Bring her round to the right, Dog Green Sector is there."

Another round came in close. Anderson yelled to his Coxswain, Frank Currier of Saugus, Massachusetts, "Get her the hell around and outta here Coxswain! Frank, for Chrissakes, get her outta here before we're all dead meat!"

As their LCVP lurched to starboard, then turned and ploughed back along its own wake, with the massive 225hp engine roaring and shaking at full throttle, Hemingway knew this was unlike anything he'd ever witnessed in Italy, Greece, Spain, or China.

A much calmer Anderson then put his hand on Currier's shoulder.

"Okay Frank, bring her around again, and then straight in between the church and that wooded inlet to your left."

Frank Currier pointed the LCVP like a missile, opened up the engine and went straight in. They hit the rise of the beach at full throttle with the ramp crashing down immediately. Officers and NCOs started barking orders as murderous German machine gun fire ripped into the GIs trying to disembark. At least two thirds died before they could move an inch, with the rest clambering over the sides of the LCVP to an almost certain death by drowning, dragged under by their heavy back packs.

Hemingway couldn't believe his eyes. Omaha Beach was a bloody shambles, with hundreds, perhaps even thousands, of dead and dying everywhere. There was no cover for the GIs. Christ Almighty, thought Hemingway, where are the bomb craters that were meant to give some sort of cover for the GIs? Some fat assed big brass in the

Air Force had probably fouled up big time. Young Americans were being slaughtered before Hemingway's eyes, he could do nothing except look and remember. For the first time in his life he felt helpless.

All he could do now was help the wounded back on board as the LCVP reversed rapidly away from the beach, its ramp closing slowly like the mouth of a huge whale feeding on human remains.

After unloading the wounded and the dead, and picking up a new cargo of GIs from the *Dorothea M. Dix*, Frank Currier headed the LCVP back toward their designated sector of Dog Green. As they approached, Hemingway could at last see through his binoculars exhausted US infantry making their way off the beach and up the bluffs behind, the fight gone, just slowly, laboriously, as though they were carrying the world on their shoulders. "Men were climbing, they were not firing, they were just moving slowly, going the other way from home."

As Hemingway continued to watch US, and Royal Navy destroyers steamed as close to Omaha Beach as they could get, "and were blowing every pillbox out of the ground with their five-inch guns. I saw a piece of a German about three feet long with an arm on it sail high up into the air in the fountaining of one shell burst." It was the end of the beginning. The worst day in the history of the American Army was nearly over.

When Hemingway returned to his room at the Dorchester Hotel in London that night he drank a bottle of Champagne and typed out one of the best pieces of war reporting he ever produced.

In the early hours of the morning of the 7th - as Martha Gellhorn stepped ashore on Omaha beach - Hemingway dreamed he was on Walloon Lake, Michigan, in his small fishing dingy with the old noisy motor. It was a fine sunny day, but he had a dreadful hangover.

Suddenly Hemingway realized he was not on Walloon Lake, but in his bed at the Dorchester. The hangover was real enough, and the noisy motor the spluttering jet engine of an approaching Doodlebug (V1 Flying Bomb) heading for the centre of London.

Then the noise stopped.

To be continued...

Going The Other Way From Home **is a fictional story of Ernest Hemingway's life and ancestry, and how his future actions were very much influenced by his, and his family's, past. The story is told from both Hemingway's point of view and from those who came into contact with him and uses actual historical narrative to help weave a fascinating account, not only of one of America's greatest writers and men, but also of his times and the people he came into contact with, such as Scott Fitzgerald, James Joyce, Gertrude Stein, Max Perkins, Morley Callaghan, J.D. Salinger and of course his wives, Hadley Richardson, Pauline Pfeiffer, Martha Gellhorn and Mary Welsh.**

Going The Other Way From Home **is a story of achievement and hope. It is a story of love and loss, of adultery, sex, vicious sustained military conflict, and of the extraordinary interrogation (virtually a military courts martial) that Hemingway had to endure in the autumn of 1944. But in the end it is a story of mental illness and suicide and also one of huge bravery, generosity and kindness that created a literary legacy second to none.**

To subscribe to this serial log on to www.humdrumming.co.uk and visit the serials section.

the organization

Guy Adams

'This is the Way the World Ends'

It all begins with the bright light, a single compressed nuclei – a singularity - beyond that, *nothing*.

Then it cracks, heat, raw energy pumping out beyond scale. The Universe *glows*. Matter and Anti-Matter collide and negate one another in the first war of creation.

In the aftermath; particles form in the cooling air, quarks for the most part, tiny flecks of potential. Then photons, neutrinos, electrons; colliding, reacting, melding with one another. Hydrogen begins to form. The initial building blocks of matter; of life. From vacuum, utter absence, to an expanding universe of proto matter. The transition takes time…

It takes nearly three minutes.

The Red Shift continues but, behind its back, small pools of gravity are beginning to form, matter rushing in on itself, building, expanding becoming more *real*, more solid. Stellar bodies; planets.

And on those planets, surfaces cool, crusts form landmasses. Within the waters, proteins and amino acids begin to consider the possibilities.

Until, after many millennia, something drags its way onto the hard surface of its brave new world and experiences its very first moment of sentience.

It thinks: "What this place needs is a fucking great McDonalds."

This is the way the world ends…

***

"Shit!" Lionel mops at the spilt ketchup on his shirt with a paper napkin and dumps the half eaten burger on the dashboard. It begins to congeal almost instantly beneath the spreading halo of coffee steam on the windscreen. David rolls his eyes and digs a pack of cigarettes out of his jacket.

"Smooth." He mutters.

"You can forget lighting one of those in my car pal." Lionel hisses, giving up on his shirt and flinging the dirty napkin over his shoulder onto the backseat.

Looking at him for a second David judges him serious and opens the passenger door with a sigh.

"Yeah, hate to fuck with the sweet pine smell of the upholstery."

"Sod the upholstery, I don't want my body pumped full of that shit." Lionel replies, tucking back into his burger, his fat lips shining with grease.

David opens his mouth and then decides life is just too damn short. He shuts the door behind him and strolls along the street, lighting his cigarette and ducking down an alley to get out of the light of the street lamps. They are, after all, supposed to be incognito. The agency expenses sheet calls it 'Undercover Surveillance', but 'Losing Your Mind With Boredom While Someone Gets Their End Away.' is far more accurate.

Working in pairs should make the job easier, but in David's experience it all depends on who you're partnered with. Lionel's conversation rarely stretches beyond sport with the occasional sideline in women. Well, their physical attributes anyway. Throwaway remarks along the lines of *'Tit's that'd make a dead man come'* or *'Arse like two boys fighting under a blanket.'* don't exactly open up conversation.

Still, ever since young Tony Morris had his head pummelled against his car bonnet by a burly husband whose powers of observation rivalled his list of affairs nobody fancies the notion of working alone.

All the thrills and spills of life in the Private Detective business.

Tom Selleck can just kiss my arse, David thinks, moving further down the alley.

He flicks his cigarette away and unzips his trouser fly, *may as well take care of business while I'm here.* Lionel believes in the judicious use of a large polystyrene coffee cup when it comes to pissing. Standard procedure if you're on your own, turning your back on the mark because your bladder is full is understandably frowned upon. Which doesn't explain why Lionel still feels the need to use the cup when David is sat next to him. He has a feeling the big man just likes it.

Maybe the risk of being beaten up isn't all that bad when you come to think about it.

There is a crash of bins from the other end of the alley followed by a bright flash of light. David curses as he wets his shoe in surprise.

Trying to keep his aim safe he glances over his shoulder, nothing in sight, whatever it is it's coming from beyond the end of the alley. Finishing, he tucks himself away and listens to what he is pretty certain is the sound of fighting.

Obviously, a sensible person would take this opportunity to carefully and considerately walk away from the possible trouble, thank whatever deity they find to their liking and stroll on. *Obviously*, that's what you would do.

David walks towards the noises, keeping to the shadows as much as possible, careful where he places his feet, not wanting to make any noise.

The alley opens out into a large courtyard, a rear access area for the buildings surrounding it. Lit by security lamps fixed high up on the walls two figures tussle in the centre.

It's theatrical this scene, gladiators in combat. They're both well dressed, suits and ties, not the expected white trash wanting to feel the breaking of bones; they would look more at home in a fashionable office or wine bar. One is clearly older than the other, moustachioed, dark and slender. The other is fair haired and broad, chubby rather than muscular.

They fight with passion, teeth clenched. Sweat and spittle glisten in the spotlights as they punch and wrestle.

The older man serves a well-placed blow to the other's jaw, the younger man rolls with it and returns with a swung fist to the gut.

It's a dance, each one anticipating the other's move, compensating for it and ready with a counter strike. They're well matched, neither showing an obvious upper hand. While each punch or kick has clear weight, the target has the ability to roll or block, round and round they go.

Then David sees something impossible.

The older man back pedals to give himself room to manoeuvre, diving to the floor and disappearing, swallowed by the tarmac with no more resistance than had he jumped into water. The younger man spins around, not surprised but alert, waiting for his opponent to reappear.

David backs away in shock, his brain trying to rationalise what he has seen and failing.

The man reappears from below, springing up through the ground and bringing the younger man's legs out from beneath him. The younger man gives a short yell and rolls along the floor, kicking out at his attacker's hand with his heel. Springing to his feet he jumps at the man and they both vanish through the tarmac only to reappear moments later erupting from the red brick of a wall several feet away.

David shakes his head subconsciously and turns to run back to the car.

There is another man standing directly behind him, his features lit briefly by the flare of his cigarette lighter: face not old but worn, hair crew-cut. He wears a leather jacket and T-Shirt, a world away from the fighting men.

"Do yourself a favour," he says, *"forget."*

***

David climbs back into the car and opens his window to let some fresh air blow away the heavy smell of fast food.

"What the hell have you been doing?" Lionel asks, "I was beginning to think you'd buggered off home or something."

"Just taking a piss." David answers, looking up at the window they're supposed to be watching.

"Took you long enough."

Lionel turns to look at his partner. The man's shaking, sweat on his forehead.

"What's wrong, you look like shit."

"Nothing." David whispers, picking up his coffee cup and tipping the last few drops into his mouth.

A strange thought is bouncing around his head but he's damned if he's going to say it out loud.

"This is the way the World ends."

To be continued…

No, no, no... You're quite wrong. Every thought or preconceived notion you have regarding authority, control, and the very *framework* of history. All of those movers, all of those shakers, did nothing.

That is the *first* great secret.

The world outside your window, so safe and secure, so perpetual, all of that hangs by a thread.

That is the *second* great secret.

The Organisation.

That is the *third* great secret.

Both a fantastical conspiracy history and an action adventure The Organisation is an ongoing serial about a secret society of temporal agents who have controlled the world for centuries. With the ability to write history and, if necessary, mould the fabric of reality itself, they have kept us on their chosen path.

Now, however, the ultimate disaster is upon us. The planet reached the point of physical collapse a few years ago and has been maintained unnaturally by The Organisation since then. Their hold, however, is slipping...

The first series of Twenty Six weekly episodes follows Organisation operatives Rathbone and Keller as they attempt to regain control over the planet, as well as standalone adventures featuring well known members of The Organisation, including:

As architect and perpetual resident of The City (a bizarre metropolis outside reality where The Organisation bases its operations), Nicholas Hawksmoor fills his days with little except fine wine and hunting out 'specialist images' on the Internet. During a particularly drunken bout of lavatorial desecration in a replica of St Paul's Cathedral he becomes aware of something else living within the deserted streets he calls home. Something that is large, vicious and definitely not supposed to be there.

As 'The man of a thousand faces' Lon Chaney Sr. was a perfect recruit for The Organisation, impersonating many figures throughout history to keep everything ticking along just as it should. During a routine mission in the seventeenth century he becomes aware of another impersonator on his trail; a man whose abilities rival his own and who will stop at nothing to disrupt planned history

Benny Goodman, Jazz King and super spy, must keep his wits about him on his mission to infiltrate the corridors of Nazi power. A rollicking 'boy's own' adventure that could only be called 'Stomping on the Fritz'!

Due to the episodic format and the wideness of its scope, there is nowhere The Organisation cannot go and no type of story it cannot tell. From horror to comedy, thriller to science fiction the only limit is several millennia of history.

To subscribe to this serial log on to www.humdrumming.co.uk and visit the serials section.

Meet The Humdrumming Crew

Meet The Humdrumming Crew

Creative Director - Lee Thompson

Lee always wanted to be a writer. He always wanted to have one of those blurbs in the back of books talking about himself and cats (in the third person, naturally).

With a distinct lack of plot-development-ability, thinking about writing a book was as far as it ever went. He decided that making things look pretty was much, much more fun.

Lee has worked on graphic design and branding projects for many major corporations (and some small ones), as well as spending a year working for the Walt Disney Company in Orlando, Florida. You know, where the sun shines.

Which he misses.

Very much.

When not chasing deadlines and doing the paperwork, Lee is our resident Cover Artist, Web Designer/Developer and Typesetter. Actually, 99% of all things graphic, go by Lee.

Surrounded by iPods, iBooks and his new 20" G5 iMac, Lee can often be found draining useless information from the interweb, fretting over whether he has enough shelf space for his forty-fifth Dalek toy, or laughing incontrollably about his workload.

Senior Editor - Guy Adams

Guy Adams collects careers like baseball cards. In his, surprisingly limited, time he has tried his hand at Museum Curator, Tour Guide, Historical Researcher, Newsagent... Seriously, he needs working on that boy.

His main occupations however have always been acting and writing. In the former he has mugged people in Emmerdale, watched Rugby in Where The Heart Is, perved around in his Y-Fronts simulating sex with a woman dressed as a horse (Genet's *The Balcony*) and earned something of a reputation by impersonating real people (Hemingway, George Bernard Shaw and Hitler to name but a few). He also toured as one half of the wittily titled Adams & Jarrett on the comedy circuit and is the youngest actor to portray Sir Arthur Conan Doyle's Sherlock Holmes professionally.

So there.

As a writer he has churned out scripts for the above comedy shows, falsified Elizabethan Mummer's Plays and works as a columnist and reviewer for Canadian Theatre E-Zine 'The Boards'. That's when he's not crowbarring every conceivable genre or style into one novel to make absurdist word soups like *More Than This* or the *Deadbeat* series.

Some of Humdrumming is unquestionably his fault.

Meet The Humdrumming Crew

Senior Editor - Stephen Newman

Steve Newman is a playwright, director, actor, historian, and freelance writer, who lives and works in Shakespeare's Stratford.

In 1997 Steve, along with two other Stratford playwrights, founded The Bird of Prey Theatre Company, which is dedicated to promoting new work. Since that time BoP has produced fourteen new plays by writers from around the world.

Steve is also a regular reviewer, feature writer, and columnist, for the Canadian theatre weekly The Boards. Steve also writes features for such magazines and newspapers as Book & Magazine Collector, Writers' Forum, Family History Monthly, Citizen Culture, and The Yorkshire Post, on such diverse people as Walt Whitman, D.H. Lawrence, T.E. Lawrence, Charles Whiting, Ernest Hemingway, and Arthur Miller.

Currently Steve is writing a history of Stratford's theatres, From Garrick to the RST, which will be available from Humdrumming in 2006. And if that wasn't enough he is, with Laurence Buxton, continuing to write Swann & Parker mysteries, with The Crime of the Crimea available soon from Humdrumming. His online serial, Ernest Hemingway: Going The Other Way From Home, is now available to read at the Humdrumming website.

Senior Editor - Laurence Buxton

Laurence Buxton was born in Worcester, England, in July 1974, and currently lives in Stratford-Upon-Avon. In 2003 he became a member of Steve Newman's Bird Of Prey Theatre Company. The subsequent experiences, both comic and dramatic, have been recounted in a diary, due for release before the end of 2005, to coincide with the publication of Cromwell: The Play.

Laurence is also collaborating with Steve Newman on a series of mystery novels, featuring the Victorian Detectives, Swann and Parker. The first, The Crime of the Crimea, will be published soon by Humdrumming.

On top of that, Laurence has also written a thriller/adventure novel, the first in a planned trilogy, called The Idol, which features a young girl from North Wales who inadvertently stumbles across a village with a dark legacy, and the life-threatening consequences of her becoming involved in it.

As a freelance writer Laurence also writes for a number of online magazines, including the Canadian theatre weekly The Boards.

Meet The Humdrumming Crew

Associate Author - James Christie

James Christie was born in the middle of a dreadful thunder storm one dark day in May back in 1947 which might explain the lifetime of turbulence he's experienced ever since.

Coming from a theatrical family he was initially trained as a musician but soon realised that while he might have had some technique he was pretty thin on talent. In the 1970's he switched careers and became – a coalman, an encyclopaedia salesman, a private investigator, a photographer (and courtesy of his Gypsy grandmother) a tarot card reader and a palmist! Working within the realms of the paranormal (he was really rather good at it and still is) he began his literary career by writing horoscopes for the local newspaper and occasional specialist articles on various aspects of the occult.

In the last six years he has published two authoritative biographies on British mediums ("Light In The Darkness" and "Out Of This World") and an in depth study of clairvoyant experiences in Spain, "In The Arms Of The Wind".

www.humdrumming.co.uk
the bit of the interweb that belongs to us.
and it looks pretty too.